THE 1976 NATIONAL CHAMPION

Pitt PANTHERS

THE 1976 NATIONAL CHAMPION

Pitt PANTHERS

Miracle on Cardiac Hill

DAVID FINOLI

THE
History
PRESS

Published by The History Press
Charleston, SC
www.historypress.com

Copyright © 2021 by David Finoli
All rights reserved

Front cover, top left: Tony Dorsett; *top center*: Al Romano; *top right*: Johnny Majors;
bottom: Pitt Stadium.
Back cover: Elliott Walker.

Unless otherwise noted, all images are courtesy of the University of
Pittsburgh Athletics.

First published 2021

Manufactured in the United States

ISBN 9781467148931

Library of Congress Control Number: 2021945993

To my granddaughters Emmy and Ellie. Your births were a shining moment that made the COVID world a much brighter place to live in.

CONTENTS

ACKNOWLEDGEMENTS

*I*n an enjoyable career of researching and writing about the teams I am most passionate about, those that represent western Pennsylvania, this book encompasses the one I hold most dear: the 1976 National Champion University of Pittsburgh Panthers football team.

Projects such as this are never complete without the incredible support of many. In this case, most important was my wonderful family, which includes my wife, Vivian; my children, Cara, Tony and Matthew and his wife, Chynna; and my three wonderful grandchildren, River, Ellie and Emmy.

My extended family has always been a source of support over the years, no matter where I've been and what I've accomplished. They have all been essential in any success I've enjoyed in my life: my brother Jamie; his wife, Cindy; my nieces Brianna and Marissa; my sister Mary; her husband, Matthew; my aunts Maryanne and Betty; and my cousins Fran, Luci, Flo, Beth, Tom, Gary, Linda, Amy, Amanda, Claudia, Ginny Lynn, Pam, Debbie, Diane, Vince and Richard; as well as the memories of my father, Domenic; my mother, Eleanor; my cousins Tom Aikens and Eddie DiLello; my Uncle Vince; my grandparents; and my aunts Louise, Norma, Jeannie, Libby, Mary and Evie. A thank-you also has to go to my in-laws, Vivian and Salvatore Pansino.

There is my round table of Pittsburgh sports experts, who provide insight when needed on the teams of today as well as those in the past. They include Chris Fletcher, Bill Ranier, Gary Kinn, Dan Russell, Rich Boyer, Shawn Christen, Matt O'Brokta, Don Lavell, Gary Degnan and

Gordon Jones turned out to be the star receiver that the experts anticipated. He caught a clutch 59-yard touchdown pass against Georgia in the 1977 Sugar Bowl that just about put the game out of reach and was selected as a First Team All-American his senior season in 1978. He finished his career as Pitt's all-time leader in receptions with 133 and is tied for eighth as of 2020. *Courtesy of the University of Pittsburgh Athletics.*

Bob Healy. Their help and enthusiasm in researching this incredible team were extremely valuable.

A thank-you also goes to the All-American kicker on the national championship team, Carson Long, who was kind enough to write the introduction for the book. His love of his team and the university they represented is always apparent.

There is the supportive team at The History Press, led by my acquisition editor, Banks Smither, and my copy editor, Rick Delaney. This is the seventh book I've done with The History Press, and their partnership in these projects has been incredible.

Finally, a thank-you to a person whose generous help in securing the photos for this book were most essential in the completion of this project: the University of Pittsburgh's tremendous executive associate athletic director, E.J. Borghetti, and also to Celeste Welsh.

INTRODUCTION

To many, including myself, the walk up Cardiac Hill, the steep street that Pitt fans took to make the trek to Pitt Stadium, was well worth it in the mid-1970s. It was an opportunity to see a program that went from the depths of college football in 1972 to a national championship four years later. It was my favorite championship season in a city that has seen so much success over the last fifty years. As well as I could wax poetic about that phenomenal accomplishment, what follows are the thoughts of its All-American kicker, Carson Long. By the time he was done with his time at Pitt, he had set the NCAA mark for most points by a kicker in a career. His words on his experiences at the school tell the story of just what this era meant for him and his teammates.

I went to Pitt for one reason. I wanted to be part of a team that could win a National Championship. So I told this to the new Pitt head football coach, Johnny Majors, in the last days of January 1973, when he came to my school and house during a fierce snowstorm. He told me then, Pitt would win a National Championship before I graduated. I believed in Coach Majors from that day forward to the present, forty-seven years later.

We enjoyed great success at Pitt. Winning seasons in 1973, 1974, 1975, and we were poised for greatness in 1976. I think about it often. Pride and enthusiasm became my bywords for the Panthers in those four

Erected in 1925, Pitt Stadium had been home to many great moments and six national championships. Perhaps the two greatest moments occurred in the Majors era. First was Tony Dorsett running for a school-record 303 yards in a 34–20 upset against Notre Dame that propelled the team into a national ranking and a spot in the Sun Bowl. The other major moment occurred a year later against Army, when it was announced that Michigan had lost to Purdue. The crowd erupted, as the news meant that Pitt was about to become the number-one team in the country. *Courtesy of the University of Pittsburgh Athletics.*

years. All of the players who came through those years still stay very close today. I believe it's part of the magic of Pitt. I made lifetime friendships with those men.

The excitement of the games at home, playing away games traveling by jet plane. Seeing for myself parts of America I couldn't have imagined when I was younger. Pitt made all of that possible, and of course the constant variable remained Coach Majors. I learned respect of authority from him, I believed in my coaches and teammates and most of all loyalty. The one game I recall most is when we beat Notre Dame at Pitt Stadium in 1975. There were still players on the team who played in 1972. I remember their faces after the game while in the locker room. Pure joy, tears of happiness of accomplishment. My last year, 1976, went the fastest. The team was built up and we were ready for the challenge and it fulfilled my dream of being a champion. I am indebted to the talented players that surrounded me for four years. The friendships that continue to this day and beyond, and I am especially grateful to my friend Johnny Majors for letting me have a small part in one of the most remarkable four years in college football history....Pitt is really it!

—Carson P. Long

Chapter 1

ROCK BOTTOM

THE DAVE HART AND CARL DEPASQUA ERAS

While Dave Hart would go on to a successful career as the athletic director at the University of Louisville and the University of Missouri, in 1968, his tenure as the head coach of the University of Pittsburgh football team was coming to an end. It was an unmitigated disaster. The Panthers finished each of their three seasons under Hart at 1-9. While consistent, it was a consistency that had dropped this once proud program to one of the worst—if not the worst—teams in major college football.

Even though Hart did deserve most of the criticism that comes with a team going 3-27 over a three-year span, he was also handcuffed with recruiting restrictions that made it difficult for even the best coaches in the country to win.

There had been two successful eras of Pitt football as the 1960s were coming to an end. The first saw two of the greatest coaches in the history of the game, Pop Warner and Jock Sutherland, stand on the Panther sideline. Between 1915 and 1938, the school won eight national championships. The second era was not to the level of the first, but between 1955 and 1963, under John Michelosen, Pitt went to two bowl games, including the 1955 Sugar Bowl, and finished third in the nation in 1963 with a 9-1 mark. Both eras ended the same way, with the school administration instituting much more stringent entrance requirements for athletes than most major college programs. This, combined with difficult intersectional schedules, proved to be a recipe for disaster.

The beginning of the steep walk to Pitt Stadium, referred to by Pitt fans as "Cardiac Hill." This angle is from DeSoto Street; at the top is the Petersen Events Center, which occupies the grounds where Pitt Stadium stood. It was often a cumbersome walk for Pitt fans, but it was worth it in the end when they got the chance to see their favorite team. *Courtesy of David Finoli.*

Following their extremely successful 1963 campaign, when a loss to Navy cost the Panthers a shot at another national title, the powers that be at the school once again decided that the football program seemed to be getting out of control when it came to academics. The school instituted stricter requirements on the football players. Edward Litchfield was the school chancellor until 1967, when he was replaced by Wesley Posvar. According to former West Virginia University sports information director Eddie Barrett, "Pitt was being run by Litchfield and Posvar and they were trying to make Pitt like an Ivy League school requiring things like two years of foreign language when, hell, English was a foreign language to many of their players."[1] Pitt also had other restrictions to deal with, such as trimesters rather than the traditional two semesters that most colleges used, and, according to Dick Fontana of *United Press International*, "a less than liberal curriculum."[2]

The athletic director at Pitt was a man by the name of Eddie Carver. He loved the game and the rivalries that came with it but was not a fan of what colleges did to win at the highest level. To try to put an end to such philosophies on winning, he helped form a group of schools, the Big Four: Pitt, Penn State, Syracuse and West Virginia. It put restrictions on how many players each school could recruit, disallowing the practice of redshirting and instituting roster limits. According to Barrett, "Carver was series and rivalry minded. He abhorred the over-ambitious Pitt program."[3]

Former WVU athletic director Leyland Byrd thought that, for "Syracuse and ourselves, we really felt it helped us because it limited the number of scholarships Pitt and Penn State could give out. It really helped with our recruiting—at least we thought so—because Pitt and Penn State could only take so many (prospects) and that left the other players available for us to recruit in Pennsylvania at that particular time. It didn't affect Penn State either way because they had so many walk-ons and they didn't need the (extra) scholarships at that point. Penn State was in between—they weren't for or against it."[4] Unfortunately for Pitt, it affected the program in a significant manner. Part of the issue was the people they put in charge of the football team. Another part was the school going above and beyond the Big Four agreement and instituting much tougher academic requirements than its nearest rivals. It was a difficult mix that pushed the extremely talented base of high school football recruits in western Pennsylvania away from their hometown school to other colleges. Changes needed to be made, but for the time being, the only thing that was changing was the head coach. To his dismay, the new Pitt athletic director, Casimir "Cas" Myslinski, was finding out that being the head coach at the University of Pittsburgh had become something that seemingly no self-respecting coaching candidate wanted.

Myslinski started his tenure at the university by being named to a search committee to find a successor to Hart. The committee also included former Pitt head coach Tom Hamilton, former Panther halfback Charles "Corky" Cost and an ex-quarterback for the school by the name of Bill Kaliden. A graduate of West Point, where he had been an All-American center under legendary football coach Earl "Red" Blaik and captain of its 1943 squad, Myslinski ran the Department of Physician Education at the United States Air Force Academy as well as being an assistant coach for the football team.

Almost a month after Hart resigned, Carver was reassigned within the university as secretary of the board of trustees. Myslinski was quickly hired as his replacement by Posvar, who had been a classmate of Myslinski at Army and worked at Air Force while the new Pitt AD was there. The committee was impressed with Cas. Posvar explained why he was hired: "He [Myslinski] pointed out a number of what I understood to be deficiencies in the way the team was being handled, and managed, and several other people who visited us made similar comments."[5]

So Casimir Myslinski was now in place as the AD as the committee set its sights on a group of coaching candidates. They included Windber, Pennsylvania's Frank Kush of Arizona State; Lloyd Easton of Wyoming; the coach of Oregon State, Dee Andros; Indiana University of Pennsylvania's (IUP) Chuck Klausing; Air Force's Ben Martin; Tom Cahill of Army; Georgie Tech defensive coordinator Dick Bestwick; three assistants under Joe Paterno: Bob Phillips, Joe McMullen and Earl Bruce; and an assistant for the Pittsburgh Steelers who won the NAIA national championship at Waynesburg, Carl DePasqua. Posvar felt the job would be one of the most prestigious in the country. The money was competitive with most coaching jobs. But when the school also decided that it would not change any of its academic requirements or rules for athletes, he quickly found out it was a position no one was interested in.

Enticed by the opportunity to reinvigorate his old hometown university and pushed on by friends who remained in the area, Kush quickly became one of Cas's main targets, along with Easton and Andros. Shortly after New Year's Day in 1969, the new Pitt AD decided that Kush was his man and made him an attractive offer. A day later, Kush accepted it. Myslinski stated, "I went looking for a winner and I found him in Frank Kush. He's a hard worker and scrapper."[6]

While Pitt decided its academic requirements would stay in place, it did bend on its redshirt policy, allowing Kush to give four redshirts, including future super-agent Ralph Cindrich, who turned out to be a superb linebacker for the Panthers.

For Cas, hiring Kush was a monumental move that could quickly turn around the fortunes of the school. Unfortunately, the joy he had at hiring Kush was only temporary. Five days after the Windber native made his decision, he changed his mind. Claiming that Tempe was a place his family felt was their new home, Kush chose to remain the head coach at Arizona State University. Whether it was for his family or because he decided the Pitt job was going to be too difficult under its academic requirements at the time, Kush's decision put Pitt back at square one. With the recruiting season quickly coming to a close and spring practice about to begin, the pressure on Cas and the hiring committee was intense.

They turned to Andros at Oregon State, but he decided to stay with the Beavers. A former assistant for the Panthers, Jack Wiley, also turned them down. As January was coming to an end, Eaton was given an offer, only to turn it down himself. The school was desperate; four offers given, four turned down. The day after the Wyoming coach said no, they turned to a former player and assistant at Pitt who had been with John Michelosen between 1955 and 1965 as a defensive assistant, Carl DePasqua. Carl had been a defensive line assistant with the Pittsburgh Steelers in 1968. Luckily, their fifth choice said yes to Myslinski.

Initially, it turned out to be an inspired choice. DePasqua won a national championship at Waynesburg in 1966 before moving on to the Steelers and would immediately be a boost to the Panther program with his infectious enthusiasm. He promised long-suffering Pitt fans improved play at his opening press conference. "I won't make any predictions but I promise you this. We'll play fundamentally sound football. We'll know how to block and tackle. We'll do our talking on the field."[7]

At first, his words came to fruition, and Pitt quickly turned around. In 1969, they improved to 4-6 before shooting out to a 5-1 mark in 1970 following impressive wins over Baylor, Kent State, Navy, West Virginia and Miami. In the WVU contest, the Panthers showed the attitude DePasqua instilled in them, coming back from a 35–8 halftime deficit to remarkably win, 36–35.

Standing at 5-1 with their first top-twenty ranking since 1963, the Panthers and the former Waynesburg coach were showing a stunned college football nation that you could compete while maintaining high academic standards. Unfortunately, the team was not deep, and it crumbled at that point as it began to suffer significant injuries. The Panthers lost their last four games of the year by a combined score of 136–48. Injuries could be blamed for the way 1970 ended, but not for what followed.

The Panthers never recovered after reaching the top twenty in 1970. While they started off with a surprising 29–25 win over UCLA at Pitt Stadium, the season quickly went downhill. Losses to Oklahoma, West Virginia, Tulane and Boston College followed, with the only high point being an exciting 36–35 win over Navy that saw the Panthers outscore the Midshipmen 26–0 in the second half after falling behind, 35–10. They ended the season winning only one of their last five contests to finish 3-8. A year later, it was even worse.

DePasqua installed the wishbone offense before the season in hopes that it would improve the Panthers' scoring ability. It did not. Playing a difficult schedule, the team started out by losing its first six contests before a 35–20 win over Boston College. The following week, it looked like things had turned around, as they were playing Syracuse tough before finally falling, 10–6. The two games turned out to be the high point, as Pitt was beaten rather easily in the final three contests by West Virginia, Navy and Penn State. The 1972 Panthers finished a disappointing 1-10. It was time again for change; the DePasqua era was coming to an end. The school needed to consider two options. Did the university need to drop the program to a minor football status and keep its high academic standards? Or would the school finally make the decision to loosen those standards, as most successful major college programs had, and take a shot at being a winner? The university chose the latter, but it knew, following its last attempt at turning around the program in 1968, that it would not be easy to lure a successful coach to Oakland.

Ten losses in one season were the most in the program's history. Myslinski met with DePasqua a week after the final game of the season, a loss to Penn State, 49–27. DePasqua had one year remaining on his $25,000-a-year, five-year contract. He was let go, and the program seemed in no better shape than it had been four years earlier, when the coach took over the program. As with Hart, it wasn't completely his fault. It is difficult to win with the stringent academic requirements in place.

If Pitt was looking to Kush again, he immediately said he wasn't interested. He confided in *Pittsburgh Press* reporter Bill Heufelder exactly why he or anyone else would be apprehensive to take the job. "No coach in the country is going to bring them instant success. The school has to take a positive approach now and say what are the other schools on our schedule doing that we have to do." Kush went on to say, "Your blue-chip athlete is looking for a reason not to come to your school. You can't afford to have things that would give him an excuse. I'm not talking about buying kids, but you've got to adapt the black and white rules that other schools go by. The idea that a good academic image will bring in kids is baloney. There's an old philosophy that they don't check your transcripts on the goal line."[8]

It was good advice that the administration needed to hear if it intended on having a winning program. The school left the Big Four and with it the stringent recruiting rules. It also dropped the foreign language requirement in an attempt to lure a successful major-college coach. There were rumors that one candidate was interested, a coach at Iowa State by the name of Johnny Majors.

Chapter 2

FINDING A SAVIOR

THE HIRING OF JOHNNY MAJORS

$\mathcal{T}$he University of Pittsburgh football team had just concluded a season in which it lost more games than any squad in the history of the program. After the embarrassment of the search to find Dave Hart's replacement, one in which Arizona State's Frank Kush had agreed to come to the school only to back out five days later, administrators had to wonder if this search would be just as difficult.

The press kept pushing Kush as a rumored candidate again, even though he flat out said he wasn't leaving Arizona State and told Pitt what they needed to do in order to hire anyone of worth. They were suggestions that the university seemed to understand at this point; their rigid academic and recruiting standards were not conducive to the kind of winning program they wanted for the school.

They immediately dropped out of the Big Four agreement they had with Penn State, West Virginia and Syracuse, an agreement that limited the scholarship offers each school could extend, made redshirting illegal and limited rosters. They also dropped the foreign language requirement and made admissions much friendlier for players the new coach would want to recruit—everything that DePasqua and Hart didn't have in their attempts to make the Panthers winners. While these changes would make the new coach's job easier, it would still be difficult to turn the program into one that could expect a winning record every season. As Kush declared, there was no way Pitt could be an instant winner.

Coach Johnny Majors signs a Pitt helmet at the Monroeville Convention Center in 2019. Coming from Iowa State in 1973, Majors promised no miracles, then went on to perform one, going 33-13-1 in four seasons. Majors took a team that statistically was the worst in the program's history at 1-10 in 1972 to an undefeated 12-0 record in 1976 as the Panthers captured their ninth national championship. *Courtesy of David Finoli.*

Unlike with the DePasqua hiring, there would be no search committee this time. It would be up to Casmir Myslinski alone to decide who the new coach would to be. Along with a new head coach, Pitt would need to replace most of the staff, although Myslinski did announce that they would be retaining the head recruiter, future head coach Serafino "Foge" Fazio, as he was considered part of Myslinski's staff and not DePasqua's.

While Cas claimed it was a tough decision to fire Carl, he stated that "we just had the wrong man for the situation. I'm not saying Carl was a bad coach. I say he's a good coach. But he just didn't fit into the pattern that we had to work with. But I think a coach has to produce under the circumstances he's put in. He knew at the time he had to produce under those circumstances."[9] DePasqua certainly didn't produce under those circumstances.

Besides Kush, the two other names being reported by the local press as potential candidates were Homer Smith, the athletic director at North Carolina, and a thirty-seven-year-old head coach who seemingly was on the list of every school looking to hire one, Iowa State's Johnny Majors. Winner of the Big Eight's Coach of the Year award in 1971, Majors had done a spectacular job resuscitating the Cyclone program, taking the team to two consecutive bowls in 1971 and 1972. Shortly after Thanksgiving, he had reportedly interviewed with Michigan State athletic director Burt Smith for their opening, and many wondered if he'd even be available by the time Myslinski talked to him.

Luckily for Cas, Michigan State hadn't made a decision, and a week later, he had the opportunity to talk to the former All-American halfback from Tennessee who finished second to Notre Dame's Paul Hornung in the 1956

Heisman Trophy vote. Rumors were swirling in the media after Majors came to Pitt for the interview that he had been offered the job.

As Christmas was coming up, Bill Heufelder exclaimed that, despite the fact that Majors had been rumored to be the replacement at many universities, he was coming to Pitt. There had been a quote from Marvin West, a writer for the *Knoxville New Sentinel*: "John Majors, it now appears, is going to Pittsburgh as the new coach of the downtrodden Panthers."[10]

The young head coach had ignored questions and interviews, wanting as little distraction as possible while preparing the Cyclones for a Liberty Bowl appearance. There was little hope of that, as the rumors began to swirl in an aggressive manner. While giving their new coach more options to recruit, Pitt also sweetened the pot financially. They reportedly would pay him $35,000 a year, one of the more lucrative salaries at the time in the country; $10,000 more than they had paid DePasqua. There was also the promise of more money with a weekly television show featuring the Panther coach.

On the day of Iowa State's Liberty Bowl appearance against Georgia Tech, the *Atlanta Constitution* reported that Majors had accepted the Panther job and signed a lucrative long-term contract. It even claimed that reliable sources quoted Majors as saying he was definitely leaving after the bowl game. Luckily for the Panther faithful, the rumors proved true, as both Pitt and Johnny Majors confirmed that he was accepting the job shortly after his Iowa State club lost to Georgia Tech in an exciting 31–30 contest.

He came to his first press conference spewing enthusiasm as members of the Pitt administration were hoping that he wouldn't back out a few days later, as Kush had done four years earlier. Listening to him at the conference certainly calmed those fears. He mentioned that while he promised no immediate miracles, he thought that this was an incredible opportunity; if it had been anything less, he would have not moved his family to Pittsburgh or asked members of his Cyclone staff to take on the challenge. He emphasized his desire to come and succeed by claiming, "we sure didn't come here to lose."[11]

It was certainly a job even he admitted he had never considered taking until now. "Out of ignorance this is one place I never had considered. I don't know anything about Pittsburgh. I visited here only two or three times years ago."[12]

Whether or not coming to Pittsburgh to coach the local major-college football team was something he intended to do, Majors was here and was about to begin what was to be one of the most incredible turnarounds in college football history. He began with giving the program a new look. In a meeting between the new coach and his returning players, he looked over at a student equipment manager who had an armful of uniforms in his hands. A shocked Majors looked at him and asked what they were. He was told they were the uniforms. They were old and worn, and Majors assumed they were practice uniforms. When told they were game uniforms, he was visibly upset. He asked why there were no names, claiming that every player deserved to have his name on the back of his jersey. He threw them in a garbage can, beginning the development of a new uniform. What is considered today the classic Pitt look—"Pitt" script on a yellowish-gold helmet with a royal blue stripe, royal blue shirt with pants the same color of the helmet and a royal blue stripe down the outside of each pant leg—began with Majors in 1973.

The school also built him a state-of-the-art weight room and an incredible new locker room in Pitt Stadium. The locker room had 147 wood open-air lockers, wall-to-wall carpeting, a new sauna, a meeting room and a reception area for the players and their families. All of these changes were made with the intention of helping the new coach entice a better grade of player to come to Pitt.

As he hit the recruiting trail, Majors made sure he communicated to the local press not to expect miracles. "I'm not going to promise you pie-in-the-sky. We've got some good players here, but not enough. We need some help."[13] It was true. If he was relying on his returning players—and he did have a couple of note, such as Dave Wannstedt—he did not have enough talent overall to compete. Luckily, that talent would soon come from the impressive group of recruits he was about to gather.

He pulled together his new coaching staff and gave them their marching orders: get as many players as possible who could help turn this program around. He had surrounded himself with a fine group of assistants. Two coaches were working for Majors for the first time: freshman head coach Bob Leahy, a former Steeler; and offensive backs coach Harry Jones, who had come from Arkansas. The rest had worked with him at one time or another at Iowa State. They included two graduate assistants, Bob Matey, the assistant freshman team coach; and Keith Schroder, the assistant in charge of scouting. His varsity staff included the following: Bobby Roper, who had served as the secondary coach with the Cyclones and now would take on the receivers at Pitt; secondary coach Joe Madden, who worked for Majors at Iowa State in 1968 before becoming the defensive coordinator at Kansas State; defensive coach Larry Holton, who also worked for Johnny early in his Iowa State tenure before becoming a defensive backfield coach at Florida State; defensive line coach Jim Dyar; offensive line coach Joe Avezzano, who eventually became the head coach at Oregon State and in the Arena Football League for the Dallas Desperados; offensive coordinator George Haffner, who enjoyed a long career as an offensive coordinator that ended in 2005 at Mary Hardin–Baylor; and defensive coordinator and assistant head coach Jackie Sherrill, Majors's number-one lieutenant at Iowa State.

Sherrill was only twenty-nine at the time but had an impressive résumé. Soon after graduating from Alabama, he began his coaching career on Paul "Bear" Bryant's staff before moving on to Arkansas. In 1968, Johnny hired him on his staff with the Cyclones, where he took over the responsibilities he would have with the Panthers. Majors also gave him the responsibility of a lifetime early on: bring to Pitt arguably the best high school running back in the country, Hopewell High School's Tony Dorsett.

DePasqua and his crew felt Dorsett was too small to be an effective major-college running back, but most others disagreed with that assessment, including Majors and Sherrill. When Sherrill went to Hopewell in order to persuade Dorsett to come to Pitt, the principal saw Sherrill talking to Tony. The principal told Sherrill that the previous Pitt staff felt the athlete was too small and that Sherrill can leave. The defensive coordinator was persistent and eventually befriended the principal. Through Sherrill's many visits to the school, Dorsett also became close to him, as did his mother, to the point where Dorsett felt like Sherrill was almost a brother.

Ed Wilamowski was a defensive end and teammate of Tony Dorsett, and the two decided they wanted to go as a package deal when college recruiters came calling. When the two visited schools, the coaches would put Wilamowski with the white players and Dorsett with the Black ones. Sherrill understood their closeness and roomed the two together when they visited Oakland.

"Ed was white and Tony was black, and at every school they visited, they were separated [in the college dorms]. I don't know if I was smarter than the others, but I didn't separate them. I knew Tony was very, very close to Ed. We kept them together," Sherrill recalled.[14] Tony later agreed that this attitude was important in his choosing Pitt, along with the fact that he had done his homework and was impressed with what Majors had done in resurrecting Iowa State's program. Eventually, both players signed with the Panthers, but it was Dorsett who was the lead in a recruiting class that four years later would be the driving force in this incredible comeback story.

With the shackles of the Big Four recruiting limitations gone, Majors brought in three times the recruits that the school had been limited to under the old pact. While many forget just how many players the staff brought in,

Outside of the Petersen Events Center is a statue of a panther, situated on the spot where Pitt Stadium used to stand. Underneath the panther is listed each number that has been retired by the school, including that of Tony Dorsett, who became the first to receive the honor in 1976 at halftime of the "Backyard Brawl." *Courtesy of the University of Pittsburgh Athletics.*

Sherrill estimated that it was seventy-six. That is a lot of freshmen, but it wasn't just the quantity that made it work. It was the quality.

Alongside Wilamowski and Dorsett, many others became stars at the school. Junior-college transfers were never an option for Pitt coaches before the 1973 season, and one of their first was one of the best. Defensive lineman Gary Burley, from Wharton Junior College in Texas, was later drafted by the Cincinnati Bengals in the third round of the 1975 NFL Draft and played nine seasons in the league and was named to the NFL All-Rookie team in 1976. Among the incoming freshmen recruited by Majors and his coaches were the phenomenal kicking tandem of placekicker Carson Long and punter Larry Swider. There was also quarterback Robert Haygood, tight end Jim Corbett, receiver Randy Reutershan and offensive linemen John Hanhauser, George Link and John Pelusi. Many future defensive standouts included Al Romano, Cecil Johnson, Don Parrish and Arnie Weatherington.

This selection of players would provide an instant burst of talent to the suffering program. For the players returning from the 1-10 club of 1972, the influx of talent and the aggressiveness to win by the new coaching staff was something of a culture shock. According to then sophomore quarterback Billy Daniels, who took over the starting spot in 1973, the off-season training program convinced many returning players that maybe this new era of Pitt football wasn't for them. "I think if Johnny brought anything to this program it was organization and enthusiasm. I'll never forget, he came and quickly started a winter workout schedule that was something none of us were prepared to undertake and many of the existing players dropped out at that point."[15]

Majors worked the players so hard, and so many left the program. The team didn't have enough players for the spring scrimmage. Majors even needed Schroeder, who hadn't played since graduating from Iowa State two years earlier, to play linebacker. The head coach recalled: "We worked them so hard at spring practice in the off season. We ran them twice a day after. I've never worked a team that hard. I worked some Iowa State teams hard and the early Tennessee teams but I never had a team work any harder than that. We had a saying, 'those who stay will play and those who stay will be champions.'"[16]

Those who stayed also endured a difficult training camp in Johnstown. The camp would show the new group of Pitt coaches which players didn't have the attitude to be champions and which players would come along for this incredible ride.

Chapter 3

1973

A MIRACLE ON ITS OWN

6-5-1

Now that Johnny Majors had become the twenty-seventh head football coach in the history of the school, he had little time to himself. Between selling the program to western Pennsylvania and recruiting, he was operating on nearly a 24/7 basis, but the former Tennessee All-American seemed to be having the time of his life. "It was fun. From six o'clock in the morning until midnight for the first two or three months I didn't have a minute to my own. I was making speeches, recruiting, going all the way around the country, and talking to everyone I could in Pittsburgh to find out what it would take to win at Pitt. I'd get into the taxicab and ask the taxi driver 'what do you think it take to win at Pitt?' I'd go downtown and I'd stop at the corner and ask a policeman, 'what do you think of Pitt, what do you think it take to win at Pitt?' I'd just wanted ideas and they said, 'coach we're behind you all the way!'"[17]

It was important for the coaching staff to take full advantage of the 1973 recruiting season. After being shackled by the twenty-five-player recruiting limit for years by the Big Four, they were free to recruit as many players as they needed. In 1974, the NCAA would pose a limit on all major-college football programs to thirty players, so it was Majors last chance to make an impact with the Panthers with as many players as he could get.

As the recruiting season was ending, the coaching staff was spread all over the country. Recruiting was expensive, and the school had just cut the

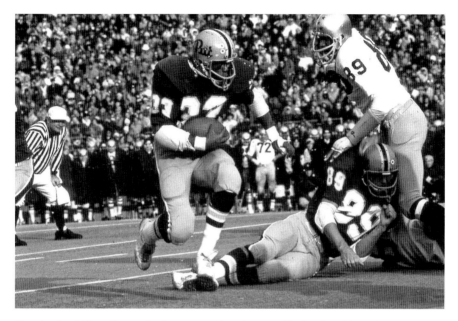

Running back Tony Dorsett looks to cut against Army at Pitt Stadium his senior season. That year, Dorsett not only became the first and still only Pitt player to win the Heisman Trophy, but he also set the single-season rushing mark with 2,150 yards. He also became the first running back in NCAA history to eclipse the 6,000-yard plateau. As of 2020, he is third all-time with 6,526 yards. *Courtesy of the University of Pittsburgh Athletics.*

athletic budget by 6 percent. Thankfully, donations, mostly from alumni, were able to fund what Majors needed.

The head coach was looking for between fifty and seventy recruits, and the day before National Letter of Intent Day, April 5, Johnny was in Florida and New York. Jackie Sherrill stayed behind to shore up his recruits in western Pennsylvania. Bob Dayar flew to Texas, Joe Madden went to New Jersey, Harry Jones took the eastern end of Pennsylvania in Philadelphia, former Steeler Bob Leahy went to Brooklyn and George Haffner was in Ohio with Keith Schroeder. Offensive line coach Joe Avezzano traveled south to both Florida and Georgia.

It wasn't enough to speak with the recruits; they had to fight off other coaches who were looking at the same players. And most of the rival schools had had more successful recent histories than the Panthers. Majors coaches were doing a great job, and on the first day, forty-two recruits sent in their letters of intent. Johnny Majors was thrilled. "Nobody's ever satisfied with the recruiting, but ours was much better than anticipated."[18] There were twenty players from the home state, including Tony Dorsett, while twenty-two came from the rest of the country. There were also three junior-college transfers in Jeff Hartin, David Spates and Thom Sindewald. Over the next couple of weeks, more letters of intent would follow. But for now, it was time for the coach to see what he had returning as spring drills began at Pitt Stadium.

As practice began, Majors announced that two more high school recruits had signed: Mark O'Toole, a quarterback from Gateway High School in nearby Monroeville, Pennsylvania; and Youngstown's John Pelusi, who the Pitt head coach claimed was the best high school center he had seen in five years. He also was thrilled to obtain the All-American junior-college transfer Gary Burley.

The returning players were put on a strenuous winter training program in an attempt not only to get them in shape but also to get them trimmed down to a proper playing weight. Eighty players came out on the Pitt Stadium turf for the first scrimmage. The defense dominated play, allowing only two scores. The offense, led by returning backup quarterback Bob Medwid, was just getting used to the I-formation offense the coaches were implementing for the upcoming season, so it wasn't surprising that the defense was outplaying them.

Despite their struggles, the coach was impressed with the efforts of his team. "I'm not going to say anything about individuals just yet or how good we're gonna be. We'll have to wait and see, but I like the spirit of this team."[19]

After three days of drills, the team took a week off to prepare for finals. Majors decided to travel to his home in Ames, Iowa, and take care of some final business there. Ames was hit with the worst snowstorm in the city's history, keeping the coach in Iowa for three extra days and giving the players some extra time off.

When the spring practice resumed, Majors continued to be impressed with the effort, but he also understood that any success he had would be because of his huge incoming recruiting class, which was now up to fifty. He also knew that he would have to see if he could plug the existing players into areas on his team that he perceived to be weak. One such player was the leading rusher from 1972, Stan Ostrowski. He had led a group of undistinguished running backs with 514 yards and a 3.6 per-rush average. He worked hard and had a good attitude. He also was a good student with a B average in pre-dentistry. But at six feet, two inches and 188 pounds, he was perhaps too tall and thin as well as not fast enough to be an effective back. Along with the fact that they had the mercurial Tony Dorsett coming in, it was apparent that Ostrowski's talents might be at another position in his

Tight end Jim Corbett was a fine all-around athlete at McDowell High School, where he won eight letters in football, basketball and volleyball. At Pitt, he started beginning midway through his freshman year and became one of the premier tight ends in the country. He was an Honorable Mention All-American his junior season before becoming an AP Second Team All-American in 1976. *Courtesy of the University of Pittsburgh Athletics.*

senior season. Majors felt that his height and good hands would make him an effective tight end. Majors proved to be correct, inserting Ostrowski as the starter over the Les Block as camp was coming to an end. As the summer went on, the lanky Ostrowski built up strength and bulk and actually lowered his 40-yard dash time to 4.7 seconds.

The culmination of spring camp, the Blue and Gold Game, was next. Johnny was making sure he was downplaying the high expectations the fans had. "If we're lucky, we could win five or six games next fall, and if we're unlucky, we could win only one. Remember, there are more strong programs than there are strong coaches. They [talking about his opening opponent Georgia] dressed maybe 120 kids for their spring game. You'll see maybe 60 at Pitt Stadium Saturday."[20]

Only five thousand fans showed up for the annual intrasquad contest as the Blue defeated the Gold, 21–7. The head coach decided to have his assistant coaches draft teams instead of using the popular format of having the first-team offense go against the second-team defense and vice versa. The two squads would then play an actual game instead of a controlled scrimmage.

Perhaps the biggest issue in the game was a lack of players. Some were on the sidelines with injuries, while others had decided that the new era of Pitt football was not for them and quit. One of the main battles at the camp was for starting quarterback, between Medwid and Daniels, who was a junior.

Medwid was listed as the starter on the depth chart following the contest, but Daniels seemed to be more consistent and caught the coach's eye.

The squad would get a break before they gathered at the University of Pittsburgh campus in Johnstown for summer camp, where the entire team, including the heralded incoming freshman class, would convene. As camp began, recruits kept signing letters of intent, with some observers estimating that Majors had accumulated approximately eighty. The players gathered at Johnstown on August 20, with the head coach and his staff intent on making this a difficult camp in order to separate those he felt could lead the program to better times from those who couldn't.

The days began at 6:15 in the intense heat that the Johnstown area had been experiencing in 1972. Sherrill, who played and worked for Paul Bryant, compared it to the famed Junction Boys summer camp when Bryant was coaching at Texas A&M, which was the feature of an ESPN film. "We did lose a few. We went to Johnstown with 3-to-5 busloads, but we didn't come back with that many. It was very, very hot, as hot as any of the camps I remember."[21]

One of those who almost left was the new running back, Tony Dorsett, who felt that it was too hot and too difficult. The young freshman was coerced into staying after "a conversation with my mom and with Jackie [Sherrill]. It was just really hard. I was pretty introverted—quiet and shy. I hid behind those big, dark sunglasses. I didn't feel like I fit in very well socially. The only time I was really comfortable was on the football field."[22]

Dorsett was coming off a fabulous performance in Hershey at the Big 33 Game, which pitted the best high school players from Ohio against the top players from Pennsylvania. It was there where Majors first realized what a tremendous talent the Hopewell running back was.

It was the first time the former runner-up to the Heisman Trophy saw Dorsett play in person. "When I saw him run in the Big 33 Game, he runs to his right and gets trapped, he reverses his field and has to give ground back to outrun three or four people, then I saw him accelerate and use a burst of speed that I never saw in my life. That night, I'd never forget. I went to my hotel room and opened the door and closed the door and like a kid I said, "Hooray we got a tail back."[23]

Once he decided to stay at camp, the young freshman was impressing everyone as much as he had impressed Majors at the game in Hershey. He was opening the eyes of everyone, including Penn State coach Joe Paterno, who said Pitt could improve to seven wins with Dorsett on the roster. Majors didn't comment on his rival's statement but did tell those who would listen that he felt this was a .500 team. The enthusiasm was up at the school; ticket sales by the end of August saw a 25 percent increase over the year before. The school also announced that the new locker room, which had been put on hold after the wooden lockers were destroyed in a fire in McKeesport, where the lockers were being built, was now on schedule to be finished by the time camp was done.

Other than Dorsett, the other main subject lines coming out of Johnstown were the battle for starting quarterback and how impressive Burley was.

Medwid, who had injured his knee and was coming back after an operation, and Daniels, who had some great moments in the spring, were locked in the battle for the starting nod along with six other competitors. Daniels had been the more consistent player at running Majors's new I-formation option offense, and Medwid never really fully recovered from his knee injury. As camp was coming to an end, it was apparent that Daniels would lead Majors first team into action. The receiving corps had been dropping too many passes, which upset Majors, but Dorsett had been spectacular, almost better than advertised.

While Dorsett was impressive, perhaps the brightest spot during the Panthers' summer camp was the defense. It looked deep and aggressive. Burley was proving to be every bit as good as Majors and Sherrill had hoped. He was more of a levelheaded talent than an emotional type. The young linebacker, who would eventually move into middle guard in Sherrill's defense, ran a 4.6-second 40-yard dash and was considered the top junior-college player in the country.

Burley seemed to have captured a starting job, as had fellow junior-college transfers David Spates and Jeff Hartin, both defensive backs. Incoming freshman Don Parrish impressed the coaches at left tackle and looked to have secured a starting spot as well.

On the final day of camp, Dorsett went head-to-head with the second-team defense in front of fifteen hundred fans. He ripped through them for an impressive 54-yard TD run down the right sideline before taking a pitchout from Daniels and rambling 74-yards for another touchdown. All told, the freshman from Aliquippa ran for 175 yards on 15 carries. Burley also played well, including a 30-yard touchdown run after blocking a Swider punt.

With the camp ending, the team was now taking shape. A few of the 141 who came to the University of Pittsburgh at Johnstown didn't return with the rest of the team. According to then-freshman tight end Jim Corbett, who would eventually became a pivotal part of the national championship squad four years later, many couldn't take the difficult camp and left.

As difficult as it was, Sherrill remembered that it was Johnny Majors's enthusiasm and personality that kept everything together. "I played for Coach Bryant and coached under Frank Broyles [at Arkansas], and Coach Majors was the best PR guy of all of them," Sherrill said. "He had a great ability to make people feel like they'd known him forever the first time they met. It's a trait that really separated Coach from 99.9 percent of the coaches out there."[24]

Majors was convinced that his first team was good enough to finish .500. While many may not have believed him after a decade of witnessing the worst era the program had produced, there was excitement in the air. Being around the new coach, it was difficult not to be excited. Everyone would get a true read of where the team stood as they traveled down to Athens, Georgia, to face Vince Dooley and the Georgia Bulldogs.

GAME ONE

THE UNIVERSITY OF PITTSBURGH PANTHERS 7
THE UNIVERSITY OF GEORGIA BULLDOGS 7
SANFORD STADIUM, ATHENS, GEORGIA
SEPTEMBER 15, 1973
RECORD: 0-0-1

As Johnny Majors prepared for his opening contest against Georgia he admitted that he hadn't seen any film of the team playing in 1972. At first, it was because there were too many other things he had to take care of. After that, he decided that there would be no purpose in watching film. The majority of the players on his team were either freshmen or junior-college transfers, so his coaches would be allowed to take a fresh approach to coaching the squad. This method made sense, but there was another situation with the 1972 squad that took the focus off the 1973 opener.

Lou Cecconi, the second-leading rusher on the previous team, was the son of Carl DePasqua'a offensive coordinator, Lou "Bimbo" Cecconi, who had been a star quarterback and halfback for the Panthers in the late 1940s. Majors wanted all of his players to record their weight after each weigh-in so they could keep track of their fluids and electrolytes, This would help to keep players from suffering heat-related issues such as heat stroke, according to the team physicians. After forgetting to record his weight on the second day of camp, Lou Jr. was given as punishment a rolling drill on the field.

Cecconi refused to do it, claiming he had an injured knee and didn't want to aggravate it. Majors heard the argument and came over, and Cecconi threw his helmet to the ground after Majors told him to either do it or go to the locker room. The senior went to the locker room and then quit the team.

Cecconi had his scholarship taken away, as with the others who had quit. He then blamed the new staff for trying to push members of the previous team off the squad, saying that he felt the volunteer trainings in the spring were actually mandatory. The players got their scholarships back when the secretary of Pitt's athletic committee, Dr. Edward Blakely, admitted that the scholarships had been taken away because of a misinterpretation of an NCAA rule and reinstated them. Majors denied Cecconi's claims and said that, while he encouraged players to attend the voluntary programs, they were not mandatory.

It was an upsetting situation, as some members of the local press were assailing the new coach for his tactics, as were some of the older players, who either quit or were demoted. But the coach was effective in focusing his squad on preparing for a tough Georgia team that had finished 7-4 the season before.

Daniels was officially named the starter at quarterback early in the week before the game because of the junior's tremendous off-season preparation. Majors also had three freshmen (Dorsett, linebacker William Leone and wide receiver Clifton Cransford) and Burley as new starters on his squad. While the enthusiasm was still there, coming off a 1-10 year, the Panthers were listed as a 15-point underdog. The fact that the man they had expected to compete for the starting quarterback job, Medwid, and their second-team tight end Les Block were missing the game with injuries didn't help the confidence of the media and fans. What they didn't realize was that all the hard work the staff and team put in since Majors was hired was about to pay off.

This team was much better prepared than expected, and the defense was just as good as advertised, if not better. It was a sweltering eighty-degree day in Athens, and 52,005 fans were cheering on the heavy favorites. Majors and Sherrill had used a 4-4-3 formation in the spring and summer but broke into a 5-2-4 formation by shifting Burley to middle guard, where he was phenomenal. This stunned Vince Dooley. Pitt limited the home team to only 230 yards of offense and 12 first downs while forcing 4 turnovers.

Offensively, Dorsett was just as good as Panther fans hoped, gaining 101 yards in his first collegiate contest. He was a force on a scoring drive in the first quarter. Starting at their 39-year line after a Bulldog punt, the

Panthers drove to the Georgia 17 with a combination of Dorsett runs and Daniels passes. At that point, the quarterback faked a pitch to the freshman and rambled down the left sideline for a touchdown that put the Panthers ahead, 7–0. They almost made it 14-0 when Mike Bulino nearly picked off a Georgia pass and had no one in front of him. It would have been an easy 85-yard return for a touchdown late in the first quarter. Instead, he dropped the ball, and the score stayed at 7–0.

Georgia tied the game in the second quarter, and then the contest turned into a titanic defensive struggle. The fans were becoming angry, booing at the Bulldogs as Pitt was outplaying them throughout most of the contest. Late in the game, the Panthers took over at their 17 and ran down the field with Dorsett leading the way, all the way to the Georgia 19 with three minutes left. Freshman Carson Long came on to try to kick a game-winner from 34 yards away. The snap from center Ray Zuraw was low, and Long missed the kick. It was the last scoring opportunity for both teams. Pitt stunned the favorites with a 7–7 tie.

Johnny Majors was euphoric. "This is perhaps the finest effort I've ever had from a football team. We didn't really know what we had—there were 15 players on the field who never had been in a major college game. I can't tell you how much this means to our program."[25] It was a stunning way to begin the Majors era at Pitt. Better times were ahead for the downtrodden program.

GAME TWO

THE BAYLOR UNIVERSITY BEARS 20
THE UNIVERSITY OF PITTSBURGH PANTHERS 14
PITT STADIUM
SEPTEMBER 22, 1973
RECORD: 0-1-1

Pitt had stunned the college football world with a 7–7 tie against Georgia, and most of the prognosticators felt that Johnny Majors would see his first Pitt victory the next week against the Baylor Bears in the home opener. They were surprised by the speed Pitt had in that contest and the incredible defense they displayed in hostile territory. It was also surprising that the young Panthers made very few mistakes.

In their opener, the Bears fell to the powerful Oklahoma Sooners, 42–14, which made the home team a touchdown favorite despite the fact that Pitt

Carson Long was a star kicker at North Schuylkill High School when Johnny Majors beat out Joe Paterno, among others, and recruited Long to Pitt. He not only quickly became the most proficient kicker in school history, but by the time he was done, Long was the all-time NCAA leader in scoring for a kicker, finishing with 268 points. He was also a UPI Second Team All-American in 1976. *Courtesy of the University of Pittsburgh Athletics.*

coaches felt Grant Teaff and his team would be coming to Pittsburgh with a chip on their shoulders. With the excitement, the Pitt ticket office was a busy place. The team was expecting a crowd of between 30,000 and 35,000 (only 28,332 showed up).

Majors was focusing on two aspects of the team. First was the punting game. It had been one of the low points in the opener, with 4 of 11 kicks under 30 yards by freshman Larry Swider. The other was an injury to an integral part of the Pitt defense that he'd need to replace. Middle guard Gary Burley, who had seemingly committed to Teaff before Majors came in and changed his mind, injured his ankle against Georgia and would not be available for the Baylor contest. The Bears coach had been professional and complementary in his response to how he felt the middle guard had been taken from him. But seeing how Burley played in the Georgia game, it certainly had to have irritated Teaff.

Johnny had to find a replacement for Burley, and freshman Don Parrish was his choice. Parrish would be responsible for stopping the Bears' speedy running back, Gary Lacy, Baylor's top rusher in 1972 and a former teammate of Burley's at Wharton Junior College. As it turned out, neither Parrish nor the rest of his teammates could stop him.

The senior tailback ran for 167 yards on 39 carries as the Baylor offensive line dominated the young Panther defense en route to a 20–14 upset victory. The Bears outrushed Pitt 323 to 174 and broke out to a 14–0 lead at the end of the first half.

Tony Dorsett, one of Pitt's lone bright spots, ran for 121 yards on 20 carries, including a magnificent 32-yard TD run early in the second half to put Pitt back in the game, 14–6. After Baylor muffed a 27-yard field goal attempt, Billy Daniels and Dorsett led Pitt downfield again, setting up a Carson Long field goal attempt from 36 yards out. Unfortunately, Long missed, as the ball traveled only to the 1-yard line, where it went out of bounds. Even though the defense had Baylor trapped deep in its zone, Teaff's offense was dominant and took the ball downfield on an eight-minute, 99-yard drive that culminated with a Lacy 1-yard run early in the final quarter to give Baylor what seemed to be an insurmountable 20–6 lead.

The Panthers cut the deficit to 6 points on a 24-yard Daniels touchdown toss to Rodney Clark, but it was too little, too late, as a frustrated Johnny Majors was still without a victory in his Pitt career. The team traveled to Evanston, Illinois, to face the Big Ten's Northwestern Wildcats the next week to see if they could rectify the situation.

GAME THREE

THE UNIVERSITY OF PITTSBURGH PANTHERS 21
THE NORTHWESTERN UNIVERSITY WILDCATS 14
DYCHE STADIUM, EVANSTON, ILLINOIS
SEPTEMBER 29, 1973
RECORD: 1-1-1

As happy as Johnny Majors was following the opening-game tie against Georgia, he was just as frustrated losing to Baylor in his first game at Pitt Stadium. He was stunned at his defense, claiming it was the softest of any team he had coached in his career to that point. He knew that not having Burley at middle guard hurt, but Don Parrish, Glen Hyde and freshman John Takacs, all of whom the coach played at the position during the game, did little to provide the impact Burley had in the opener.

He felt somewhat better after looking at the films, saying that his team's youth was the main reason for the defeat. Johnny reminded people following the game: "I was never one to build a pie-in-the-sky attitude. Remember that we inherited a 1-10 team."[26]

One of the things that caught the young squad in their second contest was overconfidence. Linebacker Kelcy Daviston, who had 36 tackles in two games, said: "Going into the game I didn't think the tie with Georgia was so much [as other people did]. I guess Georgia took us lightly and we took Baylor lightly. Our execution was poor [against Baylor]."[27]

Traveling to Evanston to face Northwestern was next on the agenda, and despite the fact that the Wildcats had been beaten, 44–0, in their opening contest against Notre Dame, Majors explained that they were a tough team and was a better passing outfit than either of Pitt's first two opponents. Northwestern's quarterback, Mitch Anderson, led the Big Ten in passing in 1972 and would be a stern test for the young Panther secondary.

While Burley's ankle was improving each day, he was questionable for the game. Parrish and return specialist and future quarterback Robert Haygood would be lost to the team in the upcoming encounter with thigh injuries. In practice, Daviston suffered a charley horse and freshman receiver Clifton Cransford hurt his ankle. Both were questionable for the contest. With Burley as well as Parrish seemingly out, two future Panther greats, Al Romano and Cecil Johnson, would get a shot at playing middle guard. Unfortunately, a key member of the offense was hurt in practice, as Tony Dorsett was hit in the thigh by an opposing defensive player's helmet. Not having Dorsett could have meant another loss. What Panther fans found out was that the small, speedy back from Hopewell was tough and would have a game for the ages against their upcoming foe.

To this point, Marshall Goldberg had been the gold standard when it came to running backs at the University of Pittsburgh. He held the all-time career yards rushing mark with 1,957 yards. No Pitt back had ever run for 1,000 yards in a year; Toby Uansa came the closest, with 964 in 1929. Only one Panther had rushed for 200 yards in a game, when Warren Heller turned the trick with exactly 200 in a 1930 contest against Penn State. In this game, Dorsett would push Heller out of the record books and show that Goldberg's and Uansa's marks were also in jeopardy.

Freshman Arnie Weatherington, who would go home to Miami in December homesick before quickly deciding Pitt was where he wanted to be, and Cecil Johnson played well while replacing the many Panther defensive casualties. It looked like it would be a replay of the Baylor game, with the Wildcats ripping through the middle of the Panther defense early on, but the young Panther middle defense toughened up and stopped Northwestern. Pitt took over, and Daniels hit Todd Toerper for 37 yards to set up a 2-yard burst by the Pitt quarterback to give the visitors a 7–0 lead.

After a Dorsett fumble set up the tying touchdown for Northwestern, the freshman running back made up for it by running for 62 yards on 8 carries in the next drive, scoring on a 6-yard run to put the Panthers ahead, 14–7. The Wildcats tied the score once again in the second period before the Aliquippa native ran for 41 yards late in the half to the opposing 21-yard line. But Long missed a field goal, and the teams went into the locker rooms tied at 14.

With 125 yards in the first half, Tony Dorsett needed only 76 to break the school single-game rushing mark. He did that and then some when he rambled down the right side for a 79-yard touchdown run that not only gave Pitt a 21–14 lead but also gave him the single-game mark.

Eventually, Dorsett would scamper for 265 yards on 38 carries, leaving Warren Heller's record far behind. The mark of 265 yards also broke the NCAA record for rushing yards in one game by a freshman, eclipsing Archie Griffin's mark of 233 a year earlier.

It was a cold and rainy day, and both defenses were dominant the rest of the way, with end Tom Perko leading the Panthers with 6 sacks as Pitt held on to the 21–14 lead for the first win in the Johnny Majors era, matching the team's win total from 1972 only three games into the season.

GAME FOUR

THE TULANE UNIVERSITY GREEN WAVE 24
THE UNIVERSITY OF PITTSBURGH PANTHERS 6
PITT STADIUM
OCTOBER 6, 1973
RECORD: 1-2-1

There was joy across the Pitt campus in Oakland as the school celebrated its first of what it hoped would be many wins in Johnny Majors's first season at the helm of the program. The team presented him with one of the game balls after the victory over Northwestern, and he gave one to Tony Dorsett and the chancellor of the school Wesley Posvar. With so many injuries and so many freshmen on the field, the head coach was ecstatic with the effort his team gave.

As good as the Panther head coach thought Dorsett could be, the freshman exceeded his thoughts. "The first I saw Dorsett was on film. I and a few other coaches sat there and watched him. I was very impressed. I was hoping—I'm a cautious optimist—I was hoping he could be what we were looking for, but I had no idea he could do what he's done at this stage. No idea whatsoever. We needed something so badly. You can't imagine how badly I wanted a player like him."[28]

While the team was thrilled to finally win, they would get a tougher test at home the following week against Tulane, who was 2-0 on the season and ranked sixteenth in the country. The Green Wave's major weapon on offense was junior quarterback Steve Foley. Foley was by far the best QB the Panthers would face to this point. He had completed 67 percent of his passes in 1973 after two contests. He led the way in the 42–0 win over Virginia Military Institute (VMI) the previous week with a 72-yard run to start the rout, adding runs of 35 and 51 yards and throwing touchdown tosses of 50 and 23 yards. For his efforts he was named, along with Dorsett, to the United Press International Backfield of the Week. Foley could do it all and was a major reason Tulane was a 3-point favorite in this affair.

The Green Wave was young and had returned most of its players from a team that crushed Pitt the year before, 33–8. Third-year coach Bennie Ellender was turning around what had been a moribund program and came into this contest relatively free of injuries. Pitt could not say the same, as Daviston and his backup, Bill Leone, were definitely out, while Burley, Parrish, Haygood and Cransford were questionable.

A small crowd of 25,054 showed up to see the Pitt defensive front line dominate the Tulane offensive line as Burley returned. He, along with Perko, Glenn Hyde, Dave Jancisin and Jim Buckmon, limited the Tulane rushing attack to a season-low 111 yards and knocked out Foley with a hit so hard that it blurred his vision. Unfortunately, no defense could overcome eight turnovers by its offense, and the Green Wave won comfortably, 24–6, despite the fact that Pitt looked like the better team on the field for most of the game.

Losing four fumbles and allowing four interceptions gave the Green Wave enough advantages, and they broke out to a 10–0 halftime lead thanks to a 41-yard TD toss from Foley and a late field goal that came after Pitt accidently touched a punt at their 17-yard line that the Green Wave jumped on. To make matters worse, Dorsett suffered a hip bruise early in the contest and spent much of the game on the bench. Despite the turnovers and injury to their star freshman, the Panthers almost went on top early in the contest after a spectacular 36-yard run by Tony and a 10-yard pass from Daniels to Toerper that appeared to be a touchdown. The referees ruled the ball on the one-foot line, giving Pitt a fourth and goal instead of six points. Tulane stopped Dorsett on the next play and took over, keeping the game scoreless.

The Panthers came back in the third quarter with a touchdown when Daniels ran the option in from 4 yards out after not finding anyone open in the end zone. They failed on the two-point conversion, but the Panthers were down by only 4 points going into the final quarter.

That was as close as Pitt got. Foley's brother Mike caught a 55-yard touchdown strike, and on a punt, Haygood lost the ball in the sun. It then hit off the Panthers' Mike Bulino deep in Pitt territory, and the Green Wave took over. They eventually ended the short drive with a 4-yard run by Ricky Hebert, giving them the 24–6 win.

Despite the fact that Pitt played well, Dorsett was limited to 77 yards rushing because of the injury. The turnovers were too much, and the team fell to 1-2-1. The season was at a crossroads, with a trip to Morgantown, West Virginia, to face their bitter rivals on the horizon.

GAME FIVE

THE UNIVERSITY OF PITTSBURGH PANTHERS 35
THE WEST VIRGINIA UNIVERSITY MOUNTAINEERS 7
MOUNTAINEER FIELD IN MORGANTOWN, WEST VIRGINIA
OCTOBER 13, 1973
RECORD: 2-2-1

There are certain games that can define a season. For Johnny Majors and his University of Pittsburgh Panthers, it was the fifth game of 1973 as they traveled the ninety-minute trip to Morgantown to face their archrivals in the "Backyard Brawl."

The Mountaineers, headed by speedy wide receiver Danny Buggs and future Hall of Fame coach Bobby Bowden, started the season by winning their first three games and garnering a spot in the top twenty, but a 28–14 loss to Indiana—a game that West Virginia was favored to win by two touchdowns—brought the Mountaineers down to earth. With the Panthers traveling to Mountaineer Field, a sellout crowd of 37,000 rabid WVU fans were expected to descend on the small stadium to hopefully give the home team the inspiration for their third consecutive victory over Pitt and sixth in their last seven games.

For the new Pitt head coach and his young team, this was the game that could make or break the season. Despite the fact that they outgained Tulane in their previous contest, 259–229, 8 turnovers by the Panthers turned what was an exciting game into a 24–6 rout, dropping them to 1-2-1 on the young campaign. A win over the Mountaineers would even Pitt's record for the year and hopefully vaulting them to a winning season. A loss would be catastrophic, leaving the Panthers with only one win at the midway point.

Much would depend on the health of Tony Dorsett, who was injured against the Green Wave and played sparingly while being held under 100 yards for the first time in his career. Buggs had also missed the previous game with a charley horse.

The Backyard Brawls had been one-sided contests over the previous six seasons. In 1970, a remarkable Pitt comeback from being down 35–8 at the half and rallying to win 36–35 was the only Panther win in that period. With WVU's dominance, many wondered if this was still a rivalry. Majors was about to remind the Mountaineers it was.

As the week went, on Dorsett seemed healthy, and the new Panther head coach was happy with the effort his team was giving on the practice field. They were as heathy as they had been all season, with only Daviston missing practice by week's end. Bowden announced that Buggs wouldn't start but was expected to play at some point in the contest. Majors made one seemingly small move that would end up being one of his most successful of the season. He moved Bruce Murphy from end to wingback. While it may not have been the main reason for the soon-to-be offensive turnaround, the team would go from averaging 12 points per game over the first four games to 24 in its last seven.

Bowden obviously was concerned with stopping Dorsett but also was impressed with the way Daniels had played at quarterback in leading Pitt's I-formation offense. While inconsistent throughout most of the season, on this Saturday, the offense was almost perfect.

Early on, the home team seemed dominant and looked like they were about to continue their mastery over Pitt. Twice West Virginia was called for interfering with a fair catch, which got the visitors out of early issues, and an illegal motion penalty against the Mountaineers negated a catch by Dave Jagdmann for significant yards.

Finally, late in the first, Pitt started from the WVU 48, and Daniels showed Bowden he was right to be concerned about him when he galloped around end for 24 yards to the 19-yard line. A personal foul when a WVU defender hit the quarterback out of bounds set Pitt up at the 10. Daniels then sprinted to his left and scored to give the visitors a 7–0 lead.

The junior quarterback scored from two yards out soon after to culminate a 75-yard drive that put the Panthers up by two touchdowns still early in the first half. After the Mountaineers cut the Panther lead in half on a 61-yard drive that was highlighted by a spectacular 44-yard completion to Buggs, it looked like West Virginia was about to tie the contest, driving to the Pitt 8-yard line. A sack by Bulino for a 13-yard loss prompted a fumble, which Rod Kirby pounced on to end the half with Pitt still up.

An incredible 35-yard run by their freshman star put Pitt back up by two touchdowns in the third. Two 12-yard TD runs by Dorsett put the game away. The second TD run came after an 81-yard interception return by Dennis Moorhead. Dorsett finished with 153 yards. Pitt won a convincing 35–7 victory.

Those who thought this rivalry was dead were wrong, as were those who assumed Pitt was falling back to its losing ways. A stretch against its eastern rivals over the next three games would prove that something special was happening at Pitt in 1973.

GAME SIX

THE UNIVERSITY OF PITTSBURGH PANTHERS 28
THE BOSTON COLLEGE EAGLES 14
ALUMNI STADIUM, CHESTNUT HILL, MASSACHUSETTS
OCTOBER 20, 1973
RECORD: 3-2-1

The Panthers' sixth game of the season was one rich in dichotomy. On one end, Boston College was the only team the 1972 Pitt squad beat, 35–20. On the other, BC was considered one of the most improved teams in the country and the toughest offensive foe Pitt would face to date.

After perhaps its greatest win of the season—a game after which the *Pittsburgh Press* sports editor called Dorsett a combination of Gayle Sayers and Greg Pruitt—the Panthers would now play a very well-rounded Eagle offense. Coach Joe Yukima was in his second season, having led Boston College to a 4-7 mark the year before. His Eagles also seemed improved, coming into this contest at 3-2, losing to Tulane, 21–16, and suffering a late loss to Miami (Florida), 15–10. With a break here or there, BC could have been 5-0. Running back Mike Esposito, one of the great power runners in the country, was averaging almost 100 yards per game. Quarterback Gary Marangi was one of the most accurate passers in the country, completing 61 percent of his passes in an era when anything over 50 percent was considered great. He had tossed only 2 interceptions in 70 attempts. Add to the mix perhaps the best field goal kicker in the country in Fred Steinfort, who was 16 for 16 in extra points and had missed only 1 of his 8 field goal attempts, and one saw why Boston College was a 7-point favorite.

It was Esposito who seemed to cause Johnny Majors the most worry. The coach hoped that his front line could handle the power back much better than they did against Tulane in week four. He would have Daviston back to help, but Rod Kirby, who had played so well against the Mountaineers, had a bad neck and was doubtful. (He would play and make a clutch defensive play, picking up a BC fumble at the 4-yard line.) Majors would also have Burley for this game, and his defensive line was coming off an incredible performance, as was his quickly improving defensive backfield. Pitt was also undefeated on the road, so he knew his young squad could handle the raucous crowd at Alumni Stadium. The other issue was whether BC could stop Dorsett, who came into the contest averaging 142.8 yards per game, second in the nation. They would soon find out that the favored Boston College squad could not stop Tony, but the Pitt defense could stop their weapons.

Pitt mustered 275 yards rushing, led by Dorsett's 109 and Billy Daniels's 71, combining for all four Panther touchdowns. The Pitt defense bottled up Esposito and the Eagles, limiting BC to only 81 yards. Pitt got the first score of day when Dorsett and Daniels ripped through the BC defense in the first quarter on a drive that ended with the Panther quarterback slicing in from the 2-yard line to give the visitors a 7–0 lead. After Kirby picked up a fumble at the four, the Eagle defense stopped the Pitt offense on fourth down at the one-foot line. But after stopping the Eagle offense, the Panthers took over the ball at the home 42 and quickly came downfield, the last 11 yards coming on a Dorsett touchdown run. Pitt was surprisingly up, 14–0.

An 85-yard flea flicker by Boston College went to the Panther 1-yard line, where Esposito took it in to cut the visitors' lead in half. But Daniels took Pitt on a 66-yard drive, which he finished by running into the end zone from the 1 to restore their 14-point lead at the half.

After the Panthers took over at the Eagle 39 in the third quarter, they quickly went downfield. Dorsett went over from the 1-yard line after Daniels was stopped twice to give Pitt a dominant 28–7 lead. Clair Wilson, who was in for the star freshman running back, lost a fumble, but the Panther front line stopped Boston College three times from within 1 yard of a first down and took over.

Boston College, which hadn't crossed midfield against the Panther defense until the final quarter, scored midway in the fourth to make it closer, but once again Pitt played a complete game against an eastern rival for another convincing victory. Now they were 3-2-1 and had a winning season for the first time since 1963 within their grasp.

GAME SEVEN

THE UNIVERSITY OF PITTSBURGH PANTHERS 22
THE NAVAL ACADEMY MIDSHIPMEN 17
PITT STADIUM
OCTOBER 27, 1973
RECORD: 4-2-1

The Pitt Panthers were quickly becoming the talk of the college football world. Only two weeks earlier, they seemed to be slipping back to their losing ways. But two important victories on the road against eastern football rivals seemed to be changing the minds of most fans and experts. Their next contest was against Navy at Pitt Stadium, a place that Johnny Majors and company had yet to win at. Undefeated on the road, Pitt had lost both contests they played at their home facility and hoped to break the streak against the Midshipmen.

Dorsett was the talk of the town, as he now had 823 yards at the halfway point of the season, only 141 yards short of Toby Uansa's single-season record. Comparisons were being made to the person who had been considered the greatest player in the program's history to this point: Marshall Goldberg. Dorsett still had a while to go to top Goldberg, who was a two-time All-American and finished third in the Heisman Trophy race in 1937 and runner-up a year later. But breaking the school single-season record and becoming the first player in Pitt history to crack 1,000 yards would be a good beginning. Tony had injured his back and had a bruised knee, but he was determined to play and keep his incredible season going.

Navy was going to be a difficult foe, coming into the contest at 3-3 after a thrashing of Air Force, 42–6. They had a talented running back of their own, as Cleveland Cooper became the first player in Navy history to eclipse the 1,000-yard plateau and helped the Midshipmen defeat the Panthers with 158 yards rushing the year before, 28–13. Their quarterback, Al Glenny, was also coming off a great contest, tossing 3 touchdowns against the Falcons.

Navy coach George Welsh was a believer that Pitt was quickly becoming one of the best football teams in the East, coming close to being on par with Penn State. "I've seen Pittsburgh from the Tulane game on and they look to me like a much-improved team. West Virginia and Boston College, Pitt played about as well as you can play against those two teams. Boston College handled us pretty easily and Pittsburgh, I thought, did about the same to them. So I would say there's no question they can play against Penn State."[29]

Success came quickly at Pitt, much quicker than it did at Iowa State, and there were rumors about other schools being interested in luring Johnny Majors away. While he was preparing for Navy, there was talk that Mississippi was interested in securing his services. He angrily denied the rumor to the press and continued his preparation to finally win a home game

Other than Dorsett, Kirby was the only other injured player, still having issues with his neck and questionable for the game. A homecoming crowd of 33,136 descended on Pitt Stadium to see the battle between two up-and-coming eastern squads on two-game winning streaks.

Freshman kicker Carson Long, who had been held without a field goal in his first six collegiate contests, had been getting help from the Steelers' Roy Gerela, and it seemed to be working. Long tied Andy Gustafson's school record of 3 field goals in one game, set in 1925. His first one, from 47 yards out, gave the home team a 3–0 lead in the first quarter. Dorsett led Pitt on an 80-yard drive in the second period with runs of 26 and 29 yards before bolting into the end zone from 1 yard out to stretch the Panther advantage to 10–0. Long belted 2 more field goals from 30 and 49 yards to increase the advantage to 16–0 at the half.

After soundly defeating WVU and Boston College and outperforming Navy in the first half, the dominance quickly ended as the Midshipmen fought back in the second half. A 4-yard run by Cooper (followed by a missed extra point) and a field goal brought Navy back to within a touchdown. With three minutes remaining and Navy possessing the ball at the Pitt 33 trying to convert on fourth down, Glenny tossed a touchdown pass to Bill Smyth, completing a 99-yard drive and bringing the visitors to within 1 point. Cooper sliced into the end zone for the 2-point conversion, giving the Midshipmen a 17–16 lead late in the contest.

Pitt had been held scoreless the entire second half, and the situation was looking tough when they took over at their own 33 in hopes of winning. Daniels took the home team on a drive down the field. Not long after the quarterback completed a pass to Jim Farley at midfield, he hit Dorsett for 16 to the Navy 29. With the Panthers quickly getting into field-goal position, Dorsett ran for 10 yards and Daniels for 15 as the Navy defense was now being dominated by the Pitt offensive line. With the ball at the 3 and time running out, Daniels faked a handoff to the Pitt freshman back and took the ball in the rest of the way to give the Panthers a dramatic 22–17 victory for their third win in a row.

Game Eight

The University of Pittsburgh Panthers 28
The Syracuse University Orangemen 14
Pitt Stadium
November 3, 1973
Record: 5-2-1

This young team was now showing that the Pitt program was on the rise. Defeating three eastern foes in a row put the Panthers within one game of clinching a .500 season. They had the opportunity to achieve that impressive feat against the Syracuse Orangemen at Pitt Stadium in the season's eighth game.

The game also had another interesting sidelight: it was an opportunity to honor Syracuse's Hall of Fame coach Ben Schwartzwalder, who was retiring at the end of the season. Schwartzwalder was in his twenty-fifth season in a career that saw him lead the school to twenty-two consecutive non-losing years, including the national championship in 1959. The program had been spiraling in the previous couple of campaigns and had a losing record in 1972, their first since 1949, Ben's first year at the university. They finished 1972 5-6, and one of their victories was against the Panthers in a close 10–6 win, which tied the all-time series at 13-13-2.

Coming into this contest, Schwartzwalder was having his worst season at the school. They stood at 0-7, and the Pitt faithful were thinking that the road to their fourth consecutive victory was pretty clear. According to head coach Johnny Majors, who was speaking with one of the heroes against Navy, kicker Carson Long, "It's a short walk from the palace to the outhouse."[30]

He knew that, while Syracuse was down, they were still capable of pulling off an upset. He was very worried about his young team's potential overconfidence, overlooking the Orangemen. While both he and Syracuse's legendary coach claimed that the Panthers had been much better than expected, Majors understood that if Pitt didn't take their winless opponents seriously, the dream season could come to a quick end. Johnny said that "no one has any reason to be satisfied. We haven't worn anybody out. We aren't world beaters."[31]

Besides Schwartzwalder's swan song at Pitt Stadium, there was something else that offered the possibility of a memorable day. Tony Dorsett stood at 928 yards, in position not only to break the school record for rushing yards in a season but also to become the first Panther to eclipse the 1,000-yard plateau.

With all the excitement, only 24,932 people showed up at Pitt Stadium to see this historic contest. Pitt was a 17-point favorite but was struggling as Syracuse ran down the field to take an early 7–0 lead. Daniels quickly led Pitt on a 90-yard drive, adeptly running through the Orangemen defense and successfully passing through it. He hit Les Block from 10 yards out to tie the score at 7–7.

Dorsett really began his historic performance on the next drive, bolting through Syracuse on a 40-yard run to their 26-yard line. The run gave the freshman 997 yards, 33 more than Toby Uansa had in 1929, a mark that had been the Pitt record for forty-four years. He then became a decoy as Daniels faked a pitch to the talented freshman and then cut inside for the touchdown that put the Panthers up, 14–7. On the next drive, Dorsett ran for 4 yards, making him the Panthers' first 1,000-yard rusher.

Early in the second half, Dorsett bolted out to what he thought would be a 69-yard touchdown run before fumbling the ball. He then went for 36 yards, setting up a 1-yard run by Dave Janasek to make it 21–7. The Pitt players were angry over what they claimed was aggressive leg-pulling by the Syracuse defense, and a brawl ensued. Order was restored quickly, but the game was all but over. Daniels rushed for a 13-yard run, giving the Panthers a 3-touchdown lead. Syracuse made it a little closer late in the game with a touchdown, but Pitt ended up winning their fourth game in a row, 28–14.

Pitts showed that it took the Orangemen seriously, running for 455 yards, led by Dorsett's 211 yards and Daniels's 165, making Ben Schwartzwalder's last trip to Pittsburgh as the Orangemen's head coach a nightmare. Pitt remarkably had clinched a .500 record after the worst season in the program's history. With Notre Dame, Army and Penn State on the schedule to end the season, the Panthers would need to sneak out a victory to make it a winning campaign.

GAME NINE

THE UNIVERSITY OF NOTRE DAME FIGHTING IRISH 31
THE UNIVERSITY OF PITTSBURGH PANTHERS 10
PITT STADIUM
NOVEMBER 10, 1973
RECORD: 5-3-1

If Majors thought the city was overconfident before the Syracuse game the week before, they were absolutely beside themselves as they were about to face the undefeated Notre Dame Fighting Irish. The Associated Press had Pitt at number twenty following the win against Syracuse, and it seemed like everyone was excited to bring on Notre Dame. But this team was much better than anyone they had faced so far in 1973.

Majors was excited about the job his junior quarterback Billy Daniels was doing. Daniels was friends with the Irish starting quarterback Tom Clements, who was also from McKees Rocks, and while Majors conceded that the Panthers didn't have the depth of Notre Dame, he thought they had some players who could match up with them.

The Panthers were healthy for the matchup. Rod Kirby was ready to come back after missing two games with a pinched nerve. Despite that fact, Notre Dame came in as a 24-point favorite. Majors would have to figure out a way to score against the number-two defense in the nation. They were giving up an average of only 63.6 yards per game, second in the nation, and 5.9 points per game, which was third. The Irish dominated every team they had played to this point, except for a 14–10 win in week three against Michigan State. Notre Dame was ranked fifth in the country.

It was certainly the biggest challenge the Panthers had to date, and the game drew a sellout crowd of 56,593. It also drew Herbie Hunt, a member of the Liberty Bowl committee who was in town looking at the home team for a potential spot in the bowl. Pitt was a formidable opponent on this day, as the Panthers humbled the Irish defense, gaining 266 yards on the ground and 117 through the air, far more than the Irish allowed on average.

Ara Parseghian and his program were introduced to Tony Dorsett, who rambled for 209 yards on the day, more than any running back had accumulated against Notre Dame in the history of the program. That would pale in comparison with what he'd accumulate two years later against them.

The Panthers eventually lost, 31–10, but the game was much closer than the score showed. The Irish vaulted ahead 7–0 in the first quarter when defensive end Jim Stock pounced on a Daniels fumble at the Pitt 24, leading to a Wayne Bullock 11-yard touchdown run. In the second quarter, the teams matched field goals, with Carson Long hitting a 34-yard attempt as time ran out to make it 10–3 at the half.

A fumble by Dave Janasek at the Irish 4 in the third quarter was quickly turned into a touchdown by Notre Dame as Bullock, who ran for 167 yards in the contest with all four Irish touchdowns, scored to make it 17–3. In the fourth, Janasek gave the Pitt faithful hope as his 1-yard TD made it 17–10.

The Pitt quarterback was right, though. The Panthers didn't have the depth of Notre Dame, who would eventually capture the 1973 national championship, as the visitors tacked on two fourth-quarter touchdowns to make the score appear more dominant than it actually was. Pitt had outgained the fifth-ranked team in the nation, 383–287, but 7 turnovers against the Irish's 1 was the stat that told the story of this game.

GAME TEN

THE UNIVERSITY OF PITTSBURGH PANTHERS 34
THE UNITED STATES MILITARY ACADEMY CADETS 0
MICHIE STADIUM, WEST POINT, NEW YORK
NOVEMBER 17, 1973
RECORD: 6-3-1

While losing their third game of the season and breaking their four-game winning streak against the soon-to-be national champion Fighting Irish of Notre Dame, Pitt proved it could play with the better programs in the country. The game was only a one-touchdown affair into the fourth quarter. The question now was whether the Panthers could avoid a letdown against a perceived weaker foe, the Army Cadets, who came into this contest winless at 0-8.

Herbie Hunt, a representative from the Liberty Bowl who had been in town looking at Pitt, said that losing to the fifth-ranked team in the nation hadn't eliminated Pitt from consideration. But he afterward mentioned that the committee would look at the national rankings before making its decision, an area that Pitt didn't fare well, in since it had dropped out of the top twenty after losing to the Irish.

While the Liberty Bowl bid seemed to be a long shot at this point, the Fiesta Bowl had contacted Pitt AD Cas Myslinski to see if he would be interested in coming to Arizona on December 21 to face the winner of the Arizona–Arizona State game, the winner of which would gain the Western Athletic Conference title. Myslinski and Majors both gave the generic answers: they had to focus on Army first, and it was up to the players. But in reality, they were thrilled at the possibility of playing in the school's first bowl since the 1956 Gator Bowl. The Peach Bowl was also interested in the Panthers and had a representative in the stands at West Point. But it appeared that the Fiesta Bowl was their best bet, as rumors were swirling that if Pitt beat Army, they would be extended a bid.

The Cadets were a 17-point underdog but had been playing better, despite the fact that they were winless. They had played well in a 19–7 loss to Miami (Florida), and their quarterback, Kingsley Fink, was one of the most accomplished Pitt had faced all season. His highlight was a 326-yard performance against Majors's alma mater, Tennessee, in the season opener.

If Johnny Majors was concerned his team was overconfident, they quickly put his fears to rest. A Fink fumble early in the contest at his own 21 led to a

5-yard touchdown run by Dorsett, who rambled for 161 yards in the contest, for a 7–0 advantage. A short 10-yard punt by Army followed, which led to a 31-yard Long field goal in a drive that was highlighted by a 24-yard pass from Daniels to Stan Ostrowski, to make the score 10–0. A 42-yard pass to a wide-open Rod Clark in the second quarter sent Pitt into the locker room at the half with a 17–0 lead.

As the second half began, Pitt was still pushing hard. A 42-yard run set up a 28-yard field goal from Long, then the freshman running back scored his second touchdown of the game to make it 27–0. Defensive back Dave Spates completed the rout when he returned an interception 86 yards in the fourth quarter, giving the Panthers a 34–0 lead.

The score remained the same as the game ended, and when the Panthers entered the locker room, they were greeted by representatives of the Fiesta Bowl, who offered the team a bid to play in their contest. Majors and the squad happily accepted the bid. The dream season was now almost complete. They clinched a winning record after a 1-10 disastrous campaign and topped it off with a bowl bid, something almost unimaginable when the season began.

There was one game left, against undefeated Penn State at State College. They'd have one game to show how they would fare against one of the best teams in the country. But even if they lost that contest, it wouldn't diminish the glory of this moment at West Point. Johnny Majors was delivering a miracle campaign.

GAME ELEVEN

THE PENN STATE UNIVERSITY NITTANY LIONS 35
THE UNIVERSITY OF PITTSBURGH PANTHERS 13
BEAVER STADIUM IN STATE COLLEGE, PENNSYLVANIA
NOVEMBER 24, 1973
RECORD: 6-4-1

With a winning record, their first since 1963, and a bowl bid in hand, the Pitt Panthers headed to State College, a place of horror for the program since Joe Paterno had taken over for Rip Engle in 1966. They were 0-7 against the Hall of Fame coach since then, losing by an average of 45–15 in the process.

While things were certainly looking up for the Panthers, Penn State came into this contest undefeated at 10-0, securing a bid to the Orange Bowl on New Year's night against LSU. Nonetheless Majors had done a phenomenal job with this young club, and most opposing coaches had respectfully acknowledged that before taking on his team. Joe Paterno apparently would not.

In a *Sports Illustrated* interview the week of the annual Pitt–Penn State contest, Paterno accused an unnamed new head coach—around thirty-seven years old, under pressure from alumni to win and being paid around $30,000—of buying players in order to succeed. He didn't name Majors, but the description made it seem like he was speaking of the Panther coach. It made sense that he would be irritated at the Tennessee alum. Majors came into an area that Paterno had recruited unchallenged for years and took Dorsett and Carson Long from him. Majors handled the situation with class, claiming that he didn't think Joe was talking about him. But while Paterno vehemently denied that he was talking about Johnny, saying it was a hypothetical situation showing the pressures of coaching, it did seem feasible that he was taking a jab at his new rival.

As the week went on, things became more civil, with Majors singing the praises of the undefeated Nittany Lions and the soon-to-be Heisman Trophy winner John Cappelletti, while Joe talked about just how good Pitt quarterback Bill Daniels was. While praising Cappelletti, Majors also said that if he had a vote for the Heisman, he'd give it to his freshman superstar, Tony Dorsett. At this point in the season, Tony had outgained his Nittany Lion opponent 1,509 to 1,361 and had given Pitt fans hope that they could pull off the upset. Despite that, Penn State was ranked sixth in the country, had the nation's top defense and came into this game as an 18-point favorite in front of a capacity crowd of 56,600 at Beaver Stadium.

Cappelletti took the challenge well, while the freshman did not. Pitt actually started out well. After the Lions went ahead 3–0 in the first quarter, Pitt dominated the second quarter, with Dorsett running in from 14 yards to give the Panthers a 7–3 lead. Then Long kicked 2 field goals, the second from 50 yards, to take a stunning 13–3 lead at the half. The field goals gave Long the school single-season record of 8, breaking Fred Cox's mark of 6 in 1962. Penn State marched downfield in the third quarter, but the drive seemed to end when quarterback Tom Shuman appeared to have been called for intentional grounding. Instead, Pitt defensive back Jeff Hartin was called for pass interference in the end zone, and the ball was placed at the 1-yard line. After the Panther defense stopped the Lions at the 1 twice, Bob Nagle finally scored. Shuman then hit Gary Hayman in the end zone for the 2-point conversion, making the score 13–11.

Pitt still held a 2-point advantage going into the fourth quarter, but they were seemingly demoralized after the turn of events. Penn State scored 24 fourth-quarter points as Cappelletti all but clinched the Heisman with 161 yards; Dorsett was held to a season-low 77 in the 35–13 defeat. While the loss hurt, for three quarters Pitt hung with the sixth-ranked team in the nation. Penn State was still the best in the East, but Pitt was now among the best in the area for the first time in a decade and would be playing in a season-ending bowl game.

Dorsett may not have won the Heisman Trophy (yet), but he was the first freshman first-team consensus All-American in twenty-nine years, running for more yards (1,586) than any freshman in the history of the game at the time. Majors would be properly recognized for taking a 1-10 program and leading it to its first winning season in ten years. He was named Coach of the Year by both the Walter Camp Foundation and the Football Writers Association of America. It truly was an amazing season that would conclude with a bowl matchup against the man who Pitt thought they had secured as their coach only five years earlier, Frank Kush.

Chapter 4

1973 FIESTA BOWL

A HUMBLING EXPERIENCE

For five days in January 1969, Frank Kush, from nearby Windber, Pennsylvania, took the reins of the football program at the University of Pittsburgh. He had had much success building the program at Arizona State and was thought to be the perfect candidate to do the same at Pitt. Unfortunately, he decided that leaving the Sun Devils was a mistake, claiming that his family considered Arizona their home. He resigned from his new assignment and returned to his post in Tempe.

The move back proved to be advantageous for both Arizona State and Kush. Since deciding not to fulfill his commitment to the Panthers, the coach led the Sun Devils to five consecutive Western Athletic Conference championships, four consecutive bowl bids, three top-ten finishes in the final Associated Press and United Press International polls and a 51-6-0 record.

Losing only to Utah, Arizona finished 1973 at 11-1 and tied for the conference crown with their main rivals, the Arizona Wildcats. In the regular-season finale, ASU thoroughly defeated the Wildcats, 55–19, securing a spot in the Fiesta Bowl against Pitt.

The Sun Devils were led by All-American quarterback Danny White, who would later be a star quarterback with the Dallas Cowboys. He was 33-4 as a starting quarterback for the Sun Devils while also doubling as the team's punter, averaging 41.7 yards per kick. He eventually would be elected to the College Football Hall of Fame and have his number 11 retired by the school. White would be the biggest challenge the young Panther secondary faced all season.

The architect of the great Pitt defense under Johnny Majors, defensive coordinator Jackie Sherrill was hired as the head coach at Washington State and missed the 1976 national championship season. He was 3-8 with the Cougars in 1976 and then was called back to Pitt after Majors accepted the head coaching job at Tennessee. Sherrill went 50-9-1 in five seasons at Pitt before moving on to Texas A&M. *Courtesy of the University of Pittsburgh Athletics.*

He was joined in the backfield by running back Benny Malone, who later enjoyed a five-year NFL career with Miami and Washington. Malone ran for 1,129 yards and 15 touchdowns, and his backfield partner Woody Green, a consensus All-American in 1972, also broke the 1,000-yard plateau, giving Kush a well-balanced offensive attack. Arizona State averaged 565.5 yards per game, which fell 1 yard short of the NCAA record the Oklahoma Sooners set in 1971.

While Majors was concerned about playing his third top-ten team in his final four games, he gave Pitt two weeks off before beginning practices. He was thrilled to see that his team was as healthy as it had been all season, with only a few players holding out of the initial practices due to the flu.

He understood how dangerous Arizona State was. He said that they were "the most explosive team in the country, the most explosive team for the last 10 years," and felt that the only way the Panthers could pull off an upset was if they "don't make mistakes, if Billy Daniels is hot in his throwing, if the receivers catch the ball, make big plays, third and nine, third and ten, to keep the drives going—not give the ball away on turnovers, two or three breaks against them."[32]

It would be a difficult task indeed to achieve those tasks, but if Majors did, there was the potential of a final top-twenty ranking and an enhanced recruiting edge. Interestingly enough, if Pitt won, Majors would receive six hundred pounds of frozen cut beef that the Arizona Beef Council was awarding to the winning coach. The school was also getting $180,000 for participating in the contest, one that only a few weeks earlier looked like they would be long shots to be playing in.

In October, when the Fiesta Bowl first laid out its list of possible opponents to play against the WAC champions, the Panthers were thirty-sixth out of forty potential teams. The NCAA had a rule that it couldn't extend bids until November 17, which the Fiesta Bowl was following. Reportedly, the other bowls had been pairing up their matchups behind the scenes. When the Fiesta began looking for opponents, it found out that many had unofficially "committed." The Fiesta tried to hit a home run by making an effort to coerce Nebraska into taking the bid, but the Cornhuskers were too successful a program to play in the relatively new bowl game and ended up going to the Cotton Bowl. Tulane and Houston were also on Fiesta's radar, but neither school was intent on going to Tempe.

Majors was enthusiastic about the potential opportunity and kept trying to sell Pitt to bowl representative Bill Shrover, whom Majors had met while he was at Iowa State. Eventually, after Fiesta was turned down by the other programs, and seeing that it would be advantageous to have a budding superstar like Tony Dorsett play in the Fiesta Bowl, they did extend a bid to Pitt.

Whether or not Pitt was the first choice, the Panthers were going to Tempe. While Johnny was getting his team ready, he was also denying rumors once again that he was entertaining an offer from Mississippi to take over its program, claiming that it was "the most ridiculous, absurd thing I've heard in a long time."[33]

Even though the rumors persisted, on the positive side, a couple of days before the game, Majors learned that he had been named Coach of the Year by the Football Writers Association of America, beating out Oklahoma's Barry Switzer, Jerry Claiborne of Maryland, Joe Paterno and Ara Parseghian.

It was a great honor for the first-year Pitt coach, but he was focused on the task at hand on the field: defeating a top-ten program in a bowl game that would be, in essence, a road game for his team, as the Panthers came into the contest a two-touchdown underdog.

As with their games against Notre Dame and Penn State, the Panthers were able to play with one of the best teams in the country for most of the contest. After the opening kickoff, on the first play of the game, Tom Perko fell on a Sun Devil fumble at the 12-yard line. Dorsett rambled for 10 yards on Pitt's opening offensive play and then shot in from the 2 on their second play to take a 7–0 lead forty-seven seconds into the contest.

An irritated White quickly hit Greg Hudson with an 18-yard completion, then threw another for 51 yards to the Pitt 3-yard line that led to a touchdown by Green to tie the game, 7–7, with 12:34 left in the first quarter. As quick as the first two touchdowns were scored, many looked forward to an offensive shootout. Instead, they were treated to a defensive standoff the rest of the first half, as the 7–7 score was maintained until a 30-yard field goal by the son of Coach Kush, Danny Kush, in the third quarter after Arizona State recovered a fumble by Daniels. That put the Sun Devils up, 10–7.

They maintained a 3-point lead until the fourth quarter, when Arizona State had a third-down-and-5 situation at their own 38. Bulino came in on a blitz and looked like he was going to sack White when the referee, who was backing up, got in the way of Bulino. White was able to get around Bulino and launched a long pass to Hudson, who pulled it in for the spectacular 62-yard touchdown to make the score 16–7 after a missed extra point.

The Panthers seemed defeated at that point and allowed 2 Green touchdowns on 23- and 1-yard runs (both extra points were missed) to make the final 28–7. Dorsett was the lone star for Pitt offensively, running for 100 of the 208 yards the Panther offense accumulated. For the Sun Devils, Hudson had 221 yards receiving and Green ran for 131 yards with 3 touchdowns.

Overall, turnovers seemed to be the most prominent feature of this contest, with Arizona State losing the ball six times and the Panthers doing so eight times.

So, the first season under Johnny Majors was now over. The team lost three of their last four games to finish 6-5-1, but the defeats were to top-ten programs. Except for fourth-quarter letdowns, Pitt showed they could play with those teams. The framework for a successful football program was now being laid, and Majors and his staff would need another phenomenal recruiting class to keep the momentum going.

Chapter 5

1974

MORE WORK TO BE DONE

7-4-0

The 1973 season was a memorable one, as Pitt rose from 1-10 in 1972 to the second-best team in the East behind Penn State. Previous coach Carl DePasqua seemingly had them to this point in 1970 when the team began the year 5-1 and ranked twentieth, but the bottom fell out after that, as they went 4-22, causing DePasqua to lose his job and giving Johnny Majors the opportunity to perform his miraculous reconstruction. Majors had the advantage of not being bogged down by the recruiting restrictions of the Big Four schools and the even stricter ones the University of Pittsburgh employed. Still, to get to the next level, Pitt had to continue to bring in elite talent, and the school would now have to abide by the NCAA limit of no more than thirty recruits a season.

Even with the new NCAA restrictions, the coaching staff brought in what was perceived to be another strong group of freshmen. There was offensive tackles Tom Brozoza and Jim Buoy, quarterback Matt Cavanaugh, defensive backs Leroy Felder and Bob Jury and halfback Elliott Walker. Walker set the single-season high school record in South Florida for yards in a season, and he became only the second back in Pitt football history to eclipse 1,000 yards, which he did in 1977. Also among the recruits was a defensive end who went on to become one of the greatest defensive players in the program's history, Randy Holloway. Holloway was one of the best players in the Western Pennsylvania Interscholastic Athletic League (WPIAL) at Sharon High School and actually was recruited as a tight end. There were

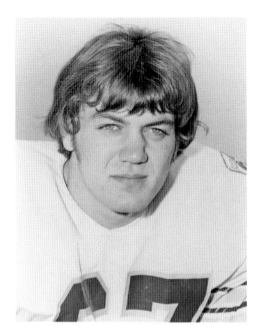

One of the greatest offensive linemen in the history of the program was Tom Brzoza. He was an All–Class A WPIAL lineman coming out of Neshannock High School in New Castle, Pennsylvania. He started his career as a guard and was named to the Football News Freshman All-American team in 1974. *Courtesy of the University of Pittsburgh Athletics.*

also two junior-college players: wide receiver Karl Farmer, who was one of the premier 440-yard sprinters in the country at Los Angeles Junior College; and Randy Cozens.

The second-year head coach was thrilled with his recruiting class. "I'm very pleased with the response we received this year. We built a foundation last year, and I'm hopeful this group will give us another floor in the building."[34] As good as the recruits were, the staff did miss out on some WPIAL stars, like running back Fred Glasgow, who went to Syracuse, and future NFL legend Joe Montana from nearby Ringgold High School, who was recruited by Notre Dame. Still, the coach claimed that he was able to sign eight of the twelve to fifteen players that he really wanted, without naming those players.

With the exceptional collection of incoming recruits to go with their returning core of players, which included eight starters on defense, it was no wonder that Pitt was appearing on some preseason top-twenty lists. The school was anticipating a huge rise in average attendance at Pitt Stadium, from 33,000 in Majors's first season to 45,000 in 1974. By mid-May, they had sold 7,549 season tickets compared to only 4,729 at the same time the season before. The ticket office was hoping to break its all-time record of 17,000 season tickets, set in 1957. They were anticipating selling between 15,000 and 20,000 tickets. Majors tempered the enthusiasm by saying, "I'm more realistic than some of our alumni who seem to feel all we need to do to better last year's record is show up. I'm confident we will have a better team than last year but that doesn't mean we'll have a better record."[35]

There were concerns on the offensive line, where Pitt returned only two starters. The loss of key seniors like Glen Hyde, Dave Wannstedt and Rod Kirby, coupled with a brutal schedule that included USC, Penn State and Notre Dame and trips to Tallahassee to face Florida State and Atlanta to take on Georgia Tech were what gave the coach concerns.

As the team was waiting to begin spring drills, two honors were bestowed on their head coach. The Dapper Dan Dinner, which celebrates the greatest sports personalities in western Pennsylvania from the previous year, honored Majors as their Man of the Year. He also was given the honor of coaching the east squad in the annual Coaches All-American All-Star Game, played in June in Lubbock, Texas. The squad also included three Pitt seniors, Jim Buckmon, Glenn Hyde and Rod Kirby. While the honors were nice, it was spring drills that the coaches were looking forward to.

Several players missed the drills due to injuries they hadn't recovered from in the previous season. They included Gary Burley, suffering from an ankle injury; Kelcy Daviston; Clifton Cransford; Dave Janasek, with a sore wrist; and Don Parrish, who was scheduled for knee surgery. While missing some key players, Majors squad returned to the gridiron and came out hitting hard, to the delight of the coaches. Dorsett picked up where he left off in 1973 by scoring three touchdowns in an early scrimmage, and quarterbacks Bob Medwid, who broke a finger on his throwing hand in the spring game, and Dave Migliore were also impressive, although they would have a difficult time moving ahead of senior Billy Daniels, who was excused for the first week of practice, as were the seventeen soon-to-be seniors, in order to get a jump on their job searches in anticipation of their post-college careers. Sophomore Robert Haygood also showed his potential by running for 174 yards in the spring game.

Even though the team started out in an enthusiastic manner, Majors became concerned as the week went on, claiming that the team was playing "ragged" and their execution was not acceptable. By the time spring practice was over, Dorsett had hurt his shoulder and Majors questioned whether or not the defensive line and the wide receivers were good enough to help Pitt take that next step. This, along with his issues on the offensive line, continued to worry Majors. The one thing that would help the Panther defensive line in 1974 was a fully healthy Gary Burley. An operation in the off-season had fixed his injured ankle, allowing the star middle guard to play on it pain-free.

Elliott Walker began his college career feeling that Johnny Majors wasn't using him enough his freshman year, and he threatened to transfer to Miami (Florida). Eventually, the situation settled down, and Majors switched to the veer offense in 1975 to get both Walker and Tony Dorsett on the field at the same time. Walker finished his career as the second-best all-time rusher at Pitt with 2,728 yards (tenth place as of 2020) and became the second Panther back to break the 1,000-yard plateau in 1977. *Courtesy of the University of Pittsburgh Athletics.*

The TV executives at ABC were questioning how good the Panthers would be. In 1974, schools had limited games on television; ABC had the lone contract for nationally broadcast Saturday contests. With Pitt's brutal schedule and questions about whether they were improved this season, ABC wanted to wait until the fourth or fifth game before it would commit to putting any Pitt games on.

While ABC was holding off on Pitt originally, there was an offer in June to have the Pitt–Penn State game moved from Pitt Stadium to Three Rivers Stadium for a Thanksgiving-evening clash that would pay each school $244,000. The reason for the move to Three Rivers was that Pitt Stadium did not have lighting to play an evening game, as ABC wanted.

Fall camp began with a fan-appreciation day at Pitt Stadium. The players then boarded buses to go to Pitt-Johnstown. There were 110 scholarship players, including the new recruits, and 20 walk-ons making the trip. Those who didn't make the trip were depth players, except for backup center Ray Zuraw, who got married and left school, and defensive back Jeff Hartin, who was found to have used up his eligibility.

The coach seemed happy that his players were apparently in good shape. And he was thrilled with the speed that was coming in with Elliott Walker, who ran a 4.4-second 40-yard dash, the same as Dorsett, and with Farmer, who ran a 4.5 40.

As camp went on, some of Pitt's players began to suffer injuries. Third-string quarterback Migliore hurt his knee, and Rodney Clark injured his ankle and was walking with the help of crutches. On the first day of contact drills, the team was aggressive, which caused many additional injuries, including to Cozens, who had what was feared to be a serious knee injury. There were also injuries to three-fourths of the starting backfield; Dorsett, Janasek and Murphy all had to sit out.

Things at Johnstown deteriorated with three days of hard rain, prompting Majors to return to Pittsburgh a day early and play the camp-ending scrimmage at Pitt Stadium. Luckily, the rash of injuries proved to be minor, as Majors and his squad escaped Johnstown without losing anyone for long periods of time.

There was clear weather on the day of the scrimmage, although it was hot. Janasek, Dorsett and Murphy returned to the lineup and played two series, with Janasek scoring on a 6-yard run and Dorsett following that up with a touchdown from 4 yards out. Weatherington was the lone injury on the day. Allen Webster surprised the coaches, with several spectacular open-field runs. Fall camp was now over, and the Panthers looked forward to facing a team that was winless in 1973: the Florida State Seminoles.

GAME ONE

THE UNIVERSITY OF PITTSBURGH PANTHERS 9
THE FLORIDA STATE UNIVERSITY SEMINOLES 6
DOAK S. CAMPBELL STADIUM, TALLAHASSEE, FLORIDA
SEPTEMBER 14, 1974
RECORD: 1-0-0

The University of Pittsburgh football program, beginning its second season under Johnny Majors, traveled south once again for an opening contest. The major difference was that, in 1973, Pitt was the prohibitive underdog against the Georgia Bulldogs. A year later, they were favored against a Florida State team coming off a winless season.

Darrell Murda had taken on the challenge of turning things around at Florida. Murda, nicknamed "Dr. Victory," had successful tenures at Adams State, North Dakota State, Arizona and Western Illinois before taking over the Seminoles. He had accumulated an impressive 106-32-2 record, capturing six conference titles in fourteen seasons. Like Majors the year before, he was confident that he had some hidden talent that he could turn into winners. But unlike the Pitt coach, he didn't have a running back like Tony Dorsett to help with the process.

Johnny was frustrated with his offense, which made little progress in its fall drills and was having issues with fumbles. Defensively, the team was improved, with a healthy Gary Burley and Don Parrish, who had signed a letter of intent to Florida State the year before but then changed his mind and came to Pitt.

With his offense struggling in practice before the season opened, Majors lauded backup quarterback Bob Medwid, whom he moved to the first-team offense in the last full scrimmage before the opener. He also praised Tony Dorsett and tight end Jim Corbett for their efforts. He had set his offensive line, the weak point of his team, with Tom Brzoza and junior Theo Lawrence starting at tackle, senior Mike Carey at center and Reynold Stoner and John Pelusi at guard. The backfield was the same. Daniels was given his starting spot at quarterback; Dorsett, Murphy and Janasek were at running back; and Toerper and Corbett were at the ends. Defensively, Tom Perko and Bill Vitalie were at the ends, Parrish and Dave Jancisin were starting at tackle, with Burley at middle guard. Two stalwarts of the 1976 national championship squad, sophomores Weatherington and Cecil Johnson, were at linebacker, while Mike Bulino, Dennis Moorhead, David

Spates and Mike Prokopovich—subbing for the injured Glenn Hodge—were in the defensive backfield.

David Spates and defensive end Ed Wilamowski were out; Wilamowski was left in Pittsburgh to recover. Most observers expected a rout; the *Pittsburgh Post-Gazette* tabbed the Panthers to win by a comfortable 30–7 margin. Majors feared it would not be an easy contest, which proved to be correct.

It was a ninety-degree, humid day that greeted the two teams. Florida State got on the board first. Thanks to the running of freshman Larry Key, who accumulated 43 yards on 5 carries, Florida State was at the Panther five when quarterback Ron Coppess hit Rudy Thomas to give the Seminoles an early 6–0 lead (they missed the extra point).

The Seminole defense was equally as efficient on the day, holding Dorsett to only 81 yards on 23 carries. The Panther offense began to move, but kicker Carson Long missed 2 field goals. Finally, with 3:30 left in the half, Dorsett bolted in from 1 yard out to tie the game, 6–6. Long missed the extra point to keep the game even.

In the third quarter, after a 31-yard kickoff return by Robert Haygood and a clutch 13-yard pass to tight end Jim Corbett, Pitt was driving when the Seminole defense sacked Daniels at the 22, setting up another field goal attempt by Long. This time, he was successful from 39 yards out to give the Panthers their first lead of the day, 9–6. It was a defensive contest the rest of the way. Both offenses were held scoreless to give Pitt a less-than-impressive 9–6 victory against the heavy underdogs. Despite that fact, Majors seemed happy with the win. "A win is a win is a win. Our defense was utterly fantastic."[36] While it wasn't the lopsided win most had envisioned, the Panthers started out the season with a victory and hoped to make it two when they traveled to Atlanta the following week.

GAME TWO

THE UNIVERSITY OF PITTSBURGH PANTHERS 27
THE GEORGIA INSTITUTE OF TECHNOLOGY YELLOW JACKETS 17
GRANT FIELD, ATLANTA, GEORGIA
SEPTEMBER 21, 1974
RECORD: 2-0-0

While Johnny Majors claimed he was happy with the performance in the opener, realistically, he had to have been bothered by an anemic offense, which garnered a mere 256 yards of total offense, only 121 yards coming on the ground. His offensive line was young, and he hoped they would improve rapidly. They would have to if they wanted to defeat Georgia Tech on the road.

The Yellow Jackets were coming off a .500 season and were now under the control of one of the most colorful coaches in the country, Frank "Pepper" Rodgers. Rodgers came from UCLA, where he claimed he didn't want to be "the guy three doors down from John Wooden's office" anymore.[37]

It would have been tough to coach under the shadow of UCLA basketball coach Wooden, but Rodgers was phenomenal and led the Bruins in a successful tenure. After starting out with a 2-7-1 mark in 1971, the Bruins were 17-5 over his final two seasons and led the nation in offense in 1973. He had been a quarterback at Georgia Tech in the early 1950s and came home to hopefully lead them to success. His opening contest came against Notre Dame, losing 31–7, before thrashing South Carolina in a game in which the Yellow Jackets set a school record with 487 yards rushing in a 35–20 win.

The Panther second-year head coach thought his club needed to learn how to play as favorites, which they didn't do well as a 21-point one the week before. Despite that, they came into this contest not only as a 3-point favorite but also tied with USC as the sixteenth-ranked team in the country in the UPI poll and fifteenth in the Associated Press, dropping three spots from the previous week.

It was Pitt's first game against Georgia Tech since playing two consecutive bowl games against them in 1955 and 1956, losing each. They had played against Rodgers, though. Three years earlier, in his first contest as the Bruin coach, Pitt handed him a 29–25 defeat.

The Panthers came into this contest with some injuries after a physical game at Florida State, with starting offensive guard John Pelusi doubtful and defensive end Ed Wilamowski, wide receiver Rodney Clark and tight end Jim Farley expected not to play.

It was a hot day in Atlanta, over eighty degrees, which translated to about one hundred degrees on the field. Dorsett looked more like the player from the year before, rambling for 168 yards on 29 carries. The defense struggled, though, against Rodgers's wishbone attack, allowing 311 yards rushing—but stopping Tech when it needed to.

Daniels got the scoring going with a 1-yard touchdown in the first quarter before the Jackets quickly tied it. Daniels led the Panthers down the field in the second quarter, hitting Farmer with his first pass of the day to the Yellow

Jacket 20. It was there that Dorsett made his most spectacular run of the day, dashing through the Tech defense to put the Panthers up again, 13–7. Long missed the extra point, and the scored remained the same at the half, as Pitt stopped a Georgia Tech drive deep in their territory and Tech missed a field goal from 40 yards out.

Early in the third quarter, the home team ripped through the Pitt defense on a 59-yard drive that put them ahead for the first time, 14–13. The Panthers came back to try to regain the lead, but the Rambling Wreck's Joe Harris picked off a Daniels pass at the 29, keeping the home team in the lead as the third quarter ended.

Dorsett then took control, running through the home team's defense. The All-American scored from 1 yard out on the first play of the fourth quarter to push Pitt back into the lead, 20–14.

Georgia Tech came back for a 33-yard field goal to cut the lead to 3 points. Then, when the Pitt offense seemed to stagnate, Larry Swider pinned Tech at its 22 with a great punt. The Panther defense held, and Dorsett once again ran through the Yellow Jacket defense to the Georgia Tech 10-yard line. At that point, Daniels pulled back on an option, getting the Yellow Jacket defense to stop, and found a wide-open Bruce Murphy in the end zone to put the final touches on a 27–17 win to push their record to 2-0.

It was a more satisfying victory than the week before. The Panthers seemed to learn how to play as a favorite.

GAME THREE

THE UNIVERSITY OF SOUTHERN CALIFORNIA TROJANS 16
THE UNIVERSITY OF PITTSBURGH PANTHERS 7
PITT STADIUM
SEPTEMBER 28, 1974
RECORD 2-1-0

After a disappointing opening contest in Tallahassee, the Pitt offense jelled in its second game, as the Panthers defeated Georgia Tech for the first time since 1920. The win vaulted them into the Associated Press top ten at number eight, and with Penn State losing to an undermanned Navy squad, 7–6, many looked at Pitt as the number-one team in the East. Coming up, though, was a potential statement game, the home opener against the University of Southern California.

USC was also having issues with its offensive line, as injures had decimated Hall of Fame coach John McKay's front line. It was the reason McKay feared his team wouldn't be national contenders and was apparent in a 22–7 opening day upset loss to Arkansas. He had a week off before this matchup against the Panthers and hoped the eighteenth-ranked ranked Trojans could figure out what they needed to do to get back on the winning track.

This would be a contest not only of two top-twenty teams but also of two of the greatest running backs college football had to offer that season— dueling ADs, if you will. Pitt had Anthony Dorsett; USC had Anthony Davis, who was looking for his third straight 1,000-yard season but had been held to only 74 yards in the team's opener.

Majors knew that the Trojans were a better and bigger team than those he had faced in his first two victories, and he also knew that McKay would be angry at the Arkansas loss and wanted to take it out on the Panthers. If McKay could get the offensive line on track, he not only had an effective running game with Davis but also one of the best quarterbacks in the nation with Pat Haden. Majors had a lot of respect for McKay, as McKay had for Majors. The USC coach thought that Johnny was the best young coach in the country.

With Pitt at 2-0 for the first time since its magnificent 1963 campaign, a place in the top ten and an enthusiastic crowd of 52,934 on hand, a win could vault the Panthers into the national championship discussion. The game meant everything to the program. When the two teams finally took the field, it was apparent that USC was the better team, by a wide margin. They rolled up 405 yards rushing as McKay quickly fixed his offensive line, compared to 99 for the Panthers. USC had 28 first downs compared to Pitt's 5. In the battle of the ADs, Davis was superior to Dorsett, with 149 yards rushing compared to the Panther sophomore's 59.

After USC broke out on top 3–0 early in the game, Bulino picked off a Haden pass at the Trojan 45. Dorsett then ran for 21 of his 59 yards on the first play of the second quarter, breaking Marshall Goldberg's school career rushing mark and bringing Dorsett's career total to 1,964, 7 ahead of Goldberg. It took Dorsett only fourteen games to surpass this much-heralded mark. The run set up a Daniels-to-Farmer touchdown pass that put Pitt up, 7–3.

The Trojans kept pushing, but the Panther defense, led by Al Romano and Randy Holloway, kept them out of the end zone. A missed USC 31-yard field goal attempt at the end of the half sent the Panthers to the locker room with a 4-point advantage.

Late in the half, Bulino hit Haden, sending the quarterback out of the game, replaced by future Trojan star Vince Evans. First downs and yards for the Panthers were rare, but USC was unable to put any points on the scoreboard. Remarkably, with the statistical dominance by the Trojans going into the fourth quarter, 4 key turnovers by USC and several great plays by the Pitt defense had the Panthers still leading the game, 7–3. With USC driving early in the final quarter, the Pitt defense once again apparently stopped the Trojans on a fourth-and-2 from the Panther 24. Unfortunately, a late hit gave USC the ball at the 13. Davis then scored three plays later to finally give the visitors the lead, 10–7.

Pitt's defense was tiring, and Evans ran the ball in from 13 yards out not long after Danny Reese intercepted a pass from Daniels deep in Panther territory. After a failed 2-point conversion, USC was ahead, 16–7, which would be the final score. The game that Pitt hoped would take them to the next level ended in disappointment.

Game Four

The University of North Carolina Tarheels 45
The University of Pittsburgh Panthers 29
Kenan Stadium, Chapel Hill, North Carolina
October 5, 1974
Record: 2-2-0

Pitt stood at seventeenth in the nation as they traveled to Chapel Hill to face the North Carolina Tarheels, but there were some troubling issues that told the tale of what actually was happening in Johnny Majors's second season in Oakland. The defense that had performed so remarkably in the opening contest against Florida State had been embarrassed on the ground against both Georgia Tech and USC. Even though he became the all-time leading rusher at the University of Pittsburgh the game before, Tony Dorsett was also struggling behind a less-than-stellar offensive line. In addition, one of Pitt's best defensive players, Mike Bulino, hurt his ankle against Southern California and would be gone from the team for the next few weeks. Mike Prokopovich, from Ambridge, got the starting call in his place.

Majors saw the issues and practiced his team hard to prepare for the upcoming game against his friend Bill Dooley, the coach of the Tarheels. The two had been assistants at Mississippi State in 1963, living next door to each other, and came into this contest with matching 2-1 marks, as North Carolina lost to Maryland, 24–12, the week before.

It was the first meeting between the two schools and was important to the success of each in the 1974 campaign. The Panther coach knew he had to retool his offensive line and was intent on doing just that. He moved junior-college transfer Pat Gleich from defensive tackle to offensive tackle, replacing Joe Stone in the starting lineup, and he moved Tom Brzoza, who was the backup at offensive tackle, to starting guard. Unfortunately, center Mike Carey had an ankle sprain and did not practice much during the week.

Defensively, Pitt would be challenged once again. The Heels had amassed 1,152 total yards in three games, compared to 680 by the Panthers. North Carolina's quarterback, Chris Kupec, had completed 71 percent of his passes, giving his team a well-balanced attack. With Burley suffering from another ankle injury, it would be even more of a challenge for Pitt.

As the game progressed in the first half, the Pitt defense was struggling once again, but the offense got off to a good start, even though Dorsett sprained his ankle, running for only 61 yards. He was out for most of the first series, but the Panthers did move the ball impressively on an 83-yard drive that ended with Dorsett running in from the 3-yard line to go up, 7–0. A 43-yard touchdown pass by Kupec quickly tied the score halfway through the first quarter.

Carolina took the lead when they pounced on a fumble by punter Larry Swider at the 2 before pushing it in for a 14–7 advantage. Haygood took the ensuing kickoff to the Heels' 48 before Daniels rolled out and ran for a touchdown on the next play to tie it once again. Pitt finally seemed to stop Carolina, but a personal foul on the Panthers as North Carolina was about to punt gave led the home team to a score that put them back ahead, 20–14.

Daniels took to the air, hitting Jim Corbett and Bruce Murphy to move the ball to the 10. The Panther quarterback then found Farmer in the left corner of the end zone for a spectacular catch, giving Pitt the halftime lead at 21–20.

The Pitt coaches had to be thrilled with the effort on the road to this point. Unfortunately, North Carolina scored 25 unanswered points in the second half to go up 45–21 before freshman Elliott Walker, who was doubtful with an injury before the contest, showed his talent with an 80-yard touchdown on his first collegiate carry and then ran it in for a 2-point conversion to make it 45–29, which is how the game ended up.

This time, there would be no false hope despite being outplayed. Pitt was outgained significantly once again, this time 552–216. At 2-2 with the

Currently, many fans criticize the University of Pittsburgh for playing in Heinz Field, claiming that an on-campus stadium would boost attendance. In 1976, the Panthers played in an on-campus stadium, Pitt Stadium, yet were having trouble averaging more than 40,000 fans early in the season, despite the fact they were competing for a national championship. One-dollar youth tickets for the game against Syracuse, plus a rivalry game against West Virginia, did improve the situation. *Courtesy of the University of Pittsburgh Athletics.*

eastern independent portion of their schedule in front of them, Majors and his staff had a huge challenge of correcting Pitt's issues. If they were unable to do that, the possibility of falling back to the losing days of the past decade was real.

GAME FIVE

THE UNIVERSITY OF PITTSBURGH PANTHERS 31
THE WEST VIRGINIA UNIVERSITY MOUNTAINEERS 14
PITT STADIUM
OCTOBER 12, 1974
RECORD: 3-2-0

In 1973, when it appeared that Pitt's season was in the balance, they faced their rivals from West Virginia University. Pitt dominated the contest, which led to a four-game winning streak and their first winning season since 1963. A year later, when it appeared that the season was once again going in a downward spiral, the Panthers faced the Mountaineers again with a victory being a necessity.

The defense in particular struggled for the second consecutive week and had the young defensive coordinator, Jackie Sherrill, frustrated. "Attitude had a lot to do with it. We didn't practice well this week and it's a lot of carryover from the Southern Cal game."[38] Linebacker Arnie Weatherington claimed: "Mentally we weren't ready for the game. I looked at everybody and nobody looked like they were ready."[39] Majors said simply it was arguably the worst performance by his team in his short tenure at the university. "It was just an old-fashioned tail-whipping. We didn't play as smart as we did in the past. I hope we learn from it."[40] He certainly hoped that the learning process would be quick. The situation might not improve, as Bulino was out with a broken ankle, defensive end Bill Vitale would sit with a knee injury and Parrish, Hodge, David Spates and Romano were all questionable with various maladies. On offense, Dave Janasek suffered from an infection in his foot and was to give way to Bobby Hutton at fullback.

One of the issues with Majors's defensive crew was the fact that the offense struggled so much in the previous two contests, causing the defense to be on the field for over 90 plays against USC and North Carolina. Part of the issue was that Dorsett was nursing an injured ankle. There was also the fact he and Daniels had several torn jerseys that had to be sewn back on the sidelines. Normally, the team had a sufficient supply of tear-away jersey replacements, but the shipment did not make it to Chapel Hill in time. To get the offense moving, Majors was considering switching from the I formation to split backs to get freshman Elliott Walker more touches, although in the end he stuck with the I formation.

Coach Bobby Bowden was not expecting the Pitt defense to come in flat as it had the previous two weeks. While the Mountaineers were also 2-2, they were coming off a 24–0 defeat of Indiana and had momentum, although their best offensive threat, Danny Buggs, was out of the contest with a calcium deposit on his thigh.

Early on, the situation appeared dire for the Panthers in front of 43,143 fans at Pitt Stadium. West Virginia went on an 80-yard drive to take a 7–0 lead, and then Bowden surprised Pitt with an onside kick that the Mountaineers recovered. Pitt held, then went 77 yards before Daniels bolted in from 1 yard out to tie the game, 7–7. In the second quarter, mental errors continued to plague the Panthers; a roughing-the-punter penalty allowed WVU to continue a drive that eventually put them ahead, 14–7. That score held up as the two teams went into the half. A tough situation had the potential to get worse, as Weatherington was ejected from the game for fighting.

At halftime, Cas Myslinski presented Dorsett with a trophy commemorating his becoming the school's all-time leading rusher. As this was happening, Majors was chastising his team in the locker room in hopes of shaking them up and ending the malaise they had been in for the last two and a half contests. Whatever he said seemed to inspire his young team.

Dorsett, who broke out of the worst slump in his short career with 145 yards on 38 carries, led the way with 31 yards, on the first drive of the second half, including the final yard to tie the game once again. It was fortuitous on that drive that the sophomore All-American fumbled the ball at the 17 to a WVU defender, only to have it bounce out of his hands and back to Dorsett. Carson Long then hit a 45-yard field goal, giving the Panthers their first lead of the contest, 17–14. It was at this point that a controversial play helped Pitt take over the game. On a fourth-and-1 at the WVU 43, Billy Daniels ran over center and, according to Bowden, did not make the first down. The referees disagreed and gave the Panthers the spot, allowing the drive to continue. Three plays later, Daniels found Farmer for a 41-yard touchdown pass to give Pitt a 10-point advantage, 24–14. The Mountaineers then failed on fourth down at their own 36, and the home team quickly went downfield, with Daniels finding Toerper from the 10 to give Pitt the important 31–14 victory.

Bowden was furious with the officials' fourth-quarter call. "We were playing good and had a chance to come from behind until they got that cheap touchdown. And the last touchdown was nothing but a gift."[41] If in fact it was a gift, it was one that Majors had been looking for, one that was the catalyst for a five-game winning streak the team was about to embark on.

GAME SIX

THE UNIVERSITY OF PITTSBURGH PANTHERS 35
THE BOSTON COLLEGE EAGLES 11
PITT STADIUM
OCTOBER 19, 1974
RECORD: 4-2-0

For the second year in a row, thanks to a victory in the Backyard Brawl, the Pitt Panthers and their fans were looking toward a bright future rather than falling back to the DePasqua days.

The Panthers would take on Boston College next, a team that came into the season with hopes of a successful year, only to be dashed by routs at the hands of both Texas and Temple. The Eagles came into Pitt Stadium at 2-2, but after defeating William & Mary the week before, the team was hoping for revenge after losing to Pitt convincingly in 1973. But they entered this contest with their most potent offensive threat, running back Mike Esposito, out with a bruised knee. For Pitt, Janasek was still out with his infected foot, as was Prokopovich with a pinched nerve in his neck.

Johnny Majors was once again toying with the idea of moving out of the I formation to a split-back offense to get his two speedy running backs, Tony Dorsett and Elliott Walker, on the field at the same time. It was the veer offense that interested Majors in the off-season, as he spent time looking at coach Bill Yeoman's version of it. The veer is an option offense that runs in a split-back formation and is effective with undersized offensive linemen who can either come in at unique angles to block or can utilize double teams on defenders.

As it turned out, Majors used both formations in the contest. The Panthers played their most effective game of the season. Dorsett finally was back to his freshman form with 191 yards on only 14 carries as Pitt thoroughly outplayed the visitors with 329 yards on the ground and 472 yards of total offense, compared to only 246 by the Eagles. Dorsett said: "I hadn't been attacking the holes like last year. That's the key for me. Yeah I've been waiting for something like this. But I never lost my confidence."[42]

Pitt broke out to an early 7–0 lead in the game before BC cut it to 7–3 with a 52-yard field goal by Fred Steinfort. An 11-yard pass from Daniels to Bruce Murphy gave the Panthers a 14–3 advantage at the half.

When the second half began, Pitt converted big plays, quickly doubling their score. First, Dorsett broke through the middle on a counter play as Eagle defenders were grabbing at his tear-away jersey, only to have pieces of it fall on the ground as he sprinted for a 61-yard touchdown run. Then Farmer sped downfield and caught a long pass from Daniels at the 15 before running it the remainder of the way for a 58-yard play to make the score 28–3.

For all intents and purposes, the game was over. After Boston College made it 28–11, Dorsett put the finishing touches on the dominant contest with a 74-yard run on a trap play up the middle to make it 35–11. It was the kind of full-game performance the team needed and showed once again that, while inconsistent, the team, when playing at its best, could be a top-twenty program.

Game Seven

The University of Pittsburgh Panthers 13
The Naval Academy Midshipmen 11
Navy–Marine Corps Memorial Stadium,
Annapolis, Maryland
October 26, 1974
Record: 5-2-0

The Pitt Panthers showed coach Johnny Majors that they were becoming the team he envisioned. "I've never had a team with this kind of speed. It's beginning to look like the team I like to see."[43] Even with the coach's enthusiasm, he remembered how difficult it was against the Midshipmen a year earlier, hanging on for a 22–17 victory after blowing a 16–0 halftime lead. Respect was there for the Panthers by second-year Navy coach George Welsh, who inferred that they were on the same level as Penn State.

While Welsh was impressed, Majors knew that the team he would go against was better than their 2-4 record indicated. They defeated Penn State earlier in the season, 7–6, and still had the academy's all-time leading runner, Cleveland Cooper, while their defense was led by the tough Chet Moeller.

Pitt was relatively healthy despite the fact that Janasek once again would not be with the team and Bulino was still out with a broken ankle. While Janasek was a solid fullback, Majors was happy with the efforts of Dorsett, Walker and Hutton against Boston College and felt he was in great shape.

Over the last two victories, Daniels hadn't thrown an interception and turnovers were held to a minimum. Against Navy, their fumbling issues resurfaced, threatening to turn their winning streak into a humbling defeat. Daniels was still solid, completing 9 of 17 with no interceptions, but the Panther running backs did their best to keep the Midshipmen in the game.

Dorsett bruised his right knee early in the game and was replaced temporarily by Walker, who ran for 21 yards on 5 carries. Once the All-American returned on the next series, he ran for 108 yards, but the backs fumbled 6 times, losing 4 of them. The turnovers kept the game at 3–0. A Carson Long 46-yard field goal in the first quarter after Parrish picked up a fumble deep in Navy territory accounted for the only points in the first half. Long hit a school record 53-yard field goal as the half ended, but a penalty was called when Pitt didn't have enough players on the line, negating the field goal.

Pitt drove deep into the Midshipmen's end of the field as the second half began, with Daniels and Dorsett accounting for 60 yards rushing, but they were stopped on the 18. Long, who was known as the "Big Edge," made it 6–0 by connecting from 35 yards. Following another fumble by Dorsett at the Pitt 28, Navy got on the scoreboard with a field goal of their own, cutting the Panther advantage to 3 points.

As the Pitt offense struggled, the defense was keeping Navy out of the end zone. Burley, who had another incredible performance, and Romano, Parrish, and Kelsy Daviston—each of whom had 2 sacks—held the Midshipmen offense to 115 yards rushing and 207 overall.

Pitt thought they had put the game away when the Panther offense finally found its way into the end zone in the fourth quarter. After a decision by Majors not to kick a field goal on a fourth-and-4 at the Midshipmen 7-yard line with 8:21 left, their speedy sophomore All-American ran for 5 yards before bolting in from the 2 to make it 13–3.

Navy finally untracked their offense late in the fourth quarter, accounting for 80 of their 207 total yards in the drive. Bob Jackson scored from 1 yard out before Navy converted the 2-point conversion to come to within 2 points at 13–11 with 1:21 remaining in the game. Remarkably, they pounced on the onside kick and had a chance to pull off what would be an unbelievable upset. Luckily, the Panther defense once again dominated the Midshipmen, pushing them from the Pitt 47 to their own 33 when they lost the ball on downs. While it was nice to move to 5-2, coming close to losing a game that shouldn't have been close was frustrating for Pitt's coach.

GAME EIGHT

THE UNIVERSITY OF PITTSBURGH PANTHERS 21
THE SYRACUSE UNIVERSITY ORANGEMEN 13
ARCHBOLD STADIUM, SYRACUSE, NEW YORK
NOVEMBER 2, 1974
RECORD: 6-2

A trend seemed to have been developing as the Panthers' season was going on. When they played on artificial turf, their speed was devastating. But playing on grass seemed to nullify the speed advantage for Pitt. They traveled to Syracuse to play the Orangemen, and Archbold Stadium had a grass field.

The trip would also be the first time Pitt played Syracuse without the Orangemen's coach, Ben Schwartzwalder, on the sidelines. There would be a new coach for the first time since 1949. The Hall of Fame coach retired following his worst campaign, as the team finished with a disappointing 2-9 mark. In his place was Frank Maloney.

Maloney came to Syracuse from Michigan, where he was an assistant for Bo Schembechler. In his tenure with the Orangemen, he had a penchant for hiring some impressive assistant coaches, such as Tom Coughlin, Nick Saban, Jerry Angelo and George O'Leary. While some of the Syracuse faithful hoped this was a new beginning for the program, they came into this contest with a 2-5 mark, defeating only Oregon State and Navy on the season. They were still primarily a running team and had played some inspired football at times, such as leading national power Penn State, 14–10, at the half before falling apart and losing, 30–14. Even though Majors stated that it would be a tough game and that Syracuse was better than the record indicated, most observers assumed that this was just press conference rhetoric and that Pitt should easily handle the home team.

Pitt was also getting Dave Janasek and Mike Bulino back, but Dorsett, Walker, Farmer, Romano, Wilamowski, Weatherington and Daviston all missed practices during the week with various injuries. Starting guard Reynold Stoner had been out with the flu. Despite that, they were a 14-point favorite in the contest.

The turf at Archbold Stadium was poor, high grass with divots on the field. Even though it was not conducive to Pitt's speed, the Panthers ran the ball through the Orangeman defense on their first series, with Dorsett accounting for 35 of the 64 yards, including the final one as they took a quick 7–0 lead. Syracuse tied it up on the strength of a 38-yard reverse by Mike Magee that led to a 2-yard TD run by Mike Bright. Carson Long had a chance to put the Panthers up by 3 points with a 52-yard attempt, but a strong wind kept it short, allowing the home team to get a field goal of their own on the next drive and giving them a 10–7 lead at the half.

The news got worse for Pitt in the third quarter, when Dorsett was lost for the game with an ankle injury. But Daniels and Bobby Hutton rose to the occasion. Daniels tossed an 18-yard pass to Murphy and a 13-yarder to Hutton before Dorsett ran for 12 on the play on which he was injured. The Panther quarterback then ran for 31 and tossed a pass to tight end Jim Corbett, who took two Syracuse defenders into the end zone. Pitt took the lead, 14–10.

A Syracuse field goal cut the lead to 14–13, but a pair of 19-yard passes from Daniels to Corbett led to a 3-yard touchdown run by Walker to give the Panthers some breathing room, 21–13. But the Orangemen weren't quite done. They drove to the Pitt 18 before defensive back Leroy Felton had an interception at the 15 to end the hopes for an upset.

Pitt's depth in the backfield was apparent. After Dorsett exited with 67 yards on 16 carries, Hutton took up the slack with 62 yards while Walker chipped in with 31. Parrish and Cecil Johnson left the game on crutches, and Farmer suffered a pulled abdomen. Despite the injuries, Pitt was now 6-2 with a game against Temple on the horizon.

Game Nine

The University of Pittsburgh Panthers 35
The Temple University Owls 24
Pitt Stadium
November 9, 1974
Record: 7-2-0

Under coach Wayne Hardin, the Temple Owls were the Pitt Panthers' major competition for second in the East, behind perennial powerhouse Penn State. Hardin was at the helm of the 1963 Navy Midshipmen, who finished second in the nation and ended Pitt's undefeated season. They had come into this contest sufffering their loss of the season to Cincinnati, 22–20, for a record of 6-1. It was also apparent that the two schools were not fond of each other.

In the preseason, Hardin had claimed that his 9-2 Owls deserved a bowl bid over Pitt and then irritated Johnny Majors by claiming he had two running backs, Henry Hynoski (the father of future Pitt running back Henry Jr.) and Tom Sloan, who were better than Tony Dorsett. It was a comment that inspired both the Pitt coach and his star back to show that Hardin was incorrect. The problem was that the sprained ankle Dorsett suffered in the Syracuse game made him questionable for the game. Despite that fact, Pitt was coming into this contest on a four-game winning streak and made another appearance in the Associate Press top twenty, coming in at nineteenth after the 21–13 win against the Orangemen.

The top-twenty appearance seemed to impress ABC-TV, which announced that it wanted the Pitt–Penn State matchup at Three Rivers Stadium for Thanksgiving evening to be broadcast to a national audience. ABC would pay each school $244,000 for the appearance. Respect was also there for Majors, as he spent the week denying rumors he was going back to his alma mater to coach Tennessee. He strongly reiterated that Pitt is where he wanted to be and that the Volunteers already had a coach. There were also rumors that Pitt was about to offer him a long-term contract.

Despite all this, Pitt still had a good Temple team to face that week, one that had been on a fourteen-game winning streak before losing to the Bearcats on the last play of the game. Led by quarterback Steve Joachim, a transfer from Penn State, Hardin and his Temple ball club were set on staking their claim for second best in the East behind the Nittany Lions. Joachim had been second in the nation in total offense and was confident he could defeat the Panthers. The rumor was that if Pitt defeated the Owls, a Sun Bowl bid was theirs—another reason for the Panthers to play their best.

Pitt was a 13-point favorite, but Dorsett would not get the opportunity to prove Hardin wrong. Hardin later backed off his statement, saying that he meant it took two of his running backs to be as productive as Tony. Dorsett's ankle was still injured, and freshman Elliott Walker got the opportunity to showcase his talent.

After Temple drove through the Pitt defense to take a 7–0 lead, Walker showed that he may be as good as both Owl backs with a dramatic 29-yard run to tie it up. Following a Temple field goal, which put the Owls up, 10–7, at the half, the Panthers took their first lead of the game when Murphy snagged a 33-yard touchdown pass from Daniels, making the score 14–10.

Hynoski, who ran for 132 yards on the afternoon and became the all-time leading rusher for Temple, bolted in from 1 yard out to give the visitors a 17–14 lead as the third quarter came to an end. Walker and Hynoski traded touchdowns, and Temple was ahead, 24–21, deep in the fourth quarter.

Just when it looked like the Owls could pull off the upset, Pitt went on a 98-yard drive that included a 41-yard run by Murphy. The young sophomore scored his third touchdown of the game to put Pitt once again in front, 28–24. Following an interception by Hodge, Walker put an exclamation point on his 169-yard performance, rambling for a 62-yard touchdown that put the game away.

Pitt hung on for an exciting 35–24 victory in front of 42,708 fans in the final contest at Pitt Stadium for the season, the end of their fiftieth year at the facility. The win unfortunately didn't impress the Sun Bowl representatives. The Panthers did not receive the bid.

GAME TEN

THE UNIVERSITY OF NOTRE DAME FIGHTING IRISH 14
THE UNIVERSITY OF PITTSBURGH PANTHERS 10
NOTRE DAME STADIUM, SOUTH BEND, INDIANA
NOVEMBER 16, 1974
RECORD: 7-3-0

Pitt was once again a nationally ranked team and would need to do something they had yet to do under Johnny Majors in order to be considered for a bowl game: beat a nationally ranked team. The Panthers were 0-4 against such teams. Their final two contests would be against Notre Dame and Penn State, and they had to defeat one in order to secure a bid. The Liberty Bowl was interested, and rumor had it that the bowl committee would extend a bid if the Panthers could defeat the Fighting Irish at South Bend.

The Irish stood at 7-1 as they prepared to host the Panthers, their lone loss being a 31–20 upset by the Purdue Boilermakers in the third game of the season. Notre Dame had a five-game winning streak of its own coming into this contest. While the Panthers moved up to seventeenth in the country, the Irish were fifth, with a bid to the Orange Bowl to play Alabama already in their pocket.

As far as their place in eastern football, Pitt rose to the top of the voting for the Lambert Trophy, the award that symbolizes the best team in the East, having beaten Penn State by 2 points and Yale by 3. Pitt would be a much more formidable opponent for the Irish than it had been in the recent past. With Walker's performance the previous week while subbing for the injured Tony Dorsett, Majors now had two potent weapons in his backfield for Ara Parseghian to prepare for. The legendary Notre Dame coach felt that the Panthers were the best offensive team he faced to this point of the season.

The coach that Parseghian would face, Johnny Majors, had a very good week leading up to the Notre Dame contest. The administration at Pitt rewarded him for his incredible job to this point with a five-year extension to his contract. Still, Pitt was a 21-point underdog to lose their eleventh straight to the Irish. Not only would they have to face Notre Dame's star quarterback, Tom Clements, a McKees Rocks native, but also, once again, they were playing on grass, a surface that seemed to nullify Pitt's great speed. Dorsett, Walker, Farmer and Romano were also suffering from injuries and hadn't practiced much during the week. On the other end, the Fighting Irish had not performed well as a big favorite. They lost to Purdue as a 30-point favorite and failed to beat the spread against Rice and Navy when they came in as 24- and 25-point favorites, respectively.

Pitt fans were excited, and while the game wouldn't be shown on national TV, it would be available as a closed-circuit broadcast at both the Syria Mosque and Soldiers and Sailors Hall in Oakland. Many Panther fans took advantage of the opportunity. What they saw was Notre Dame dominate Pitt on the field statistically, outgaining Pitt by a 374–198 margin in yards gained. They also saw the end of the Billy Daniels era at the school. The senior quarterback tore cartilage in his knee on a trick play, a pass to him from Dorsett in the second quarter, and was out for the remainder of the season. Tony Dorsett was held to only 61 yards while trying to run on a very slippery field. The Irish's Wayne Bullock, more of a power runner, rambled for 124. Despite the dominance statistically, backup quarterback Bob Medwid helped keep the game close.

After falling behind in the first quarter, 7–0, Medwid led the Panthers on a drive late in the second and scored the tying touchdown on a fourth-and-goal from the 1-yard line, and the teams went into the locker room tied. Carson Long, who missed a 57-yard attempt in the first half, put the Panthers ahead after Hodge recovered a fumble by Clements with a 52-yard kick that hit off the goalpost then went through for a 10–7 lead.

The fifth-ranked Fighting Irish, who had 3 turnovers that kept Pitt in the game, answered with a touchdown to surge back ahead late in the contest, 14–10. While the touchdown should have ended the upset bid for the underdog Panthers, Medwid led them down the field for a potential game-winning touchdown as time was running out. An 18-yard pass to Rodney Clark put them at the 17. Then, after a motion penalty pushed the Panthers back to the Notre Dame 22, Medwid missed Murphy in the end zone with eleven seconds left. He then thought he had the game-winning TD to Farmer, but defensive back Reggie Barnett came over at the last possible second to knock it away on a fabulous play. Medwid misfired on the game's final play to allow the home team to escape with a 14–10 win.

With the loss, Pitt once again failed to beat a top-twenty team and lost out on a Liberty Bowl bid. But Majors was proud of the effort, as this game was the end to the domination Notre Dame had over the Panthers during the previous decade.

GAME ELEVEN

THE PENN STATE UNIVERSITY NITTANY LIONS 31
THE UNIVERSITY OF PITTSBURGH PANTHERS 10
THREE RIVERS STADIUM
NOVEMBER 28, 1974
RECORD: 7-4-0

Since Joe Paterno had come to the Nittany Lions as their head coach, Penn State had completely embarrassed the Panthers every time the two schools met. Johnny Majors had brought the program back to respectability, and the game had now become relevant for the first time since 1963, signified by the fact that ABC had the game moved to Three Rivers Stadium in Pittsburgh. The stadium's lights made the game a Thanksgiving-night national television event. While this game would be for the Lambert Trophy, emblematic of football supremacy in the East, the question still remained: Could Pitt play a competitive game against a Paterno-led team?

For the University of Pittsburgh, switching the game from the Saturday before Thanksgiving at Pitt Stadium to Three Rivers on Thanksgiving night meant a $244,000 payday that the athletic department couldn't pass up. Penn State had already collected $415,000 on previous TV appearances before taking its $244,000 share. It was a payday that turned an athletic department that was losing money into one that was profitable. The other advantage that playing in the four-year-old facility had for the Panthers was that the Astroturf would showcase their impressive speed.

While Pitt was hoping to improve with an eighth victory, Tony Dorsett was hoping for a positive end to what had been a disappointing season. After an All-American freshman season, he was still short of the 1,000-yard plateau, with 939 yards going into the contest. A new offensive line was part of the problem for his decline, as was the injuries Dorsett suffered through the season. Losing Billy Daniels at quarterback against Notre Dame with torn ligaments in his knee was also an issue. He was the best quarterback on the roster, despite the fact that Medwid, his replacement, played effectively against the Irish. Majors was confident in Medwid, claiming, "I'm sad because we lost Daniels, but I'm happy we've got someone as competent as Medwid backing him up."[44] Paterno chipped in. "Bob Medwid and Steve Joachim were the best quarterbacks in the state when they were seniors in high school. We recruited Joachim and that's one of the reasons Medwid didn't come to Penn State."[45]

Paterno stated that beating Pitt was more important to him than going to a bowl game. The series was now tied at thirty-five wins apiece with three ties, thanks to Joe leading the Nittany Lions to eight straight victories against their rivals. But he was concerned about this contest, especially the Panther defense led by Gary Burley, who Paterno called the greatest defensive player he had ever faced to that point in his career.

The weather was cold coming into the contest. Pitt had to cancel a practice at the stadium because the turf was frozen. Tenth-ranked Penn State was a touchdown favorite over the eighteenth-ranked Panthers as the cold weather continued into game night. The game started off with Pitt staying with the Lions through the first half. After a 50-yard Chris Bahr field goal to put Penn State up, 3–0, Dorsett went in from 2 yards out in the second quarter to put the Panthers ahead, 7–3. Bahr was able to tack on a second 3-pointer, but Pitt still had the lead at the half, 7–6.

In the second half, the Lions scored 10 unanswered points to make the score 16–7 before Long cut the lead to 6 points with a 40-yard field goal. That, unfortunately, was the closest the Panthers came.

Bahr hit his fourth field goal of the game in the fourth, then kicked off to Pitt. Allen Webster fumbled the kickoff close to the goal line, and the Lions' Tom Williams fell on it in the end zone for a touchdown to give Penn State a 25–10 advantage. They tacked on one more touchdown to turn a close game into a rout, 31–10.

For Paterno and his team, it was the ninth win in the row over the Panthers. Penn State had a trip to the Cotton Bowl in the near future. For Pitt, it was the sixth loss in a row to a top-twenty team under Majors, although Tony Dorsett did run enough to break the 1,000-yard plateau once again. Pitt won one more game than it had the year before, but the Panthers were staying home for the holidays after a disappointing ending.

Chapter 6

1975

TURNING THE CORNER

8-4-0

As Johnny Majors was beginning his third season at the University of Pittsburgh, the roster of players he recruited was now the major component of his squad. There were only thirteen seniors on the team, three of whom contributed in 1974: Karl Farmer, who was recruited by Majors out of junior college; Tom Perko; and Dennis Moorhead. Majors had only twelve returning starters.

Perhaps the two most important areas Majors would have to restructure with his returning players was once again the offensive line, where only Tom Brzoza and Joe Stone returned, and at quarterback, where Robert Haygood and Matt Cavanaugh would battle to replace Billy Daniels. Daniels was joining the coaching staff as a graduate assistant. Neither Haygood nor Cavanaugh had ever thrown a varsity pass before.

The third-year Panther coach also had another big change on the horizon for the Pitt offense. He was officially switching from the I formation to the veer offense. The veer, as explained in the previous chapter, highlighted a team's speed. This would be particularly advantageous for a team that had three speedy backs in Tony Dorsett, who was coming off his second straight 1,000-yard season; Elliott Walker, who had a 6.8 yards per carry average his freshman campaign; and Bobby Hutton, who had improved his blocking skills as a fullback and ran a 4.6 40-yard dash. "I'm concerned about changing the offense from the I to the veer but that's something we

When receiver Gordon Jones was recruited by Pitt out of nearby East Allegheny High School, he was considered one of the jewels of their recruiting class. Many called him the "Tony Dorsett of his position." Jones won seven letters at East Allegheny in football, basketball and track and was selected All-State by both the Associated Press and United Press International. *Courtesy of the University of Pittsburgh Athletics.*

have to do. The veer suits our personnel best. We have speed and we have good running backs," Majors said.[46]

At quarterback, Haygood seemed to be the best option for the veer, as he was a great runner with good speed. Cavanaugh showed some skill running while adding a passing component to the formation. But while he had the stronger arm and was an effective runner, he was not the equal of Haygood.

Defensively, the team had to replace some talent, including All-American Gary Burley, who was a third-round selection in the NFL draft by Cincinnati. Only six of eleven starters returned, but it was a talented core that included Perko, Cecil Johnson, Don Parrish and Arnie Weatherington. What was concerning was the fact that the defense that had been so effective in 1973 had a disappointing 1974 campaign, as many teams ran effectively against it. Overall, the defense gave up 2,505 yards rushing, compared to 2,039 the season before. But the core of Pitt's national championship defense got the opportunity to start and put those concerns to rest.

To get the team to the next level, Majors and his staff needed to continue to bring in exceptional high school talent. The 1975 recruiting class would in fact be talented, as twenty-nine players joined the program. They included Ralph Still, recruited as a quarterback but would go on to be an effective wide receiver; tackle Jim Morsillo; tackle Matt Carroll; linebacker Al Chesley; Jeff Delaney, brought in as a halfback but would go on to greatness at Pitt as a defensive back; defensive tackle David Logan; and Gordon Jones, from nearby East Allegheny High School, who went on to be one of the greatest receivers in the program's history. Eight of the recruits were All-Americans: Chesley, Jones, Morsillo, Still, Steve Gautad, Raymond Harris, Al Papay and Harold Cook.

As the off-season went on, Majors was named as the head coach of the north squad in the American Bowl, a game that featured the best seniors of 1974. Burley, Mike Carey and Mike Bulino were representing the university at the game. Those three players had meant a lot to their head coach in his first two years at Pitt.

Also in the off-season an unfortunate situation had developed. Elliott Walker was reportedly unhappy at Pitt and threatened to transfer to Miami (Florida), according to Miami sportswriter Bill Brubaker. Majors admitted that the soon-to-be-sophomore running back was homesick but said that he didn't expect Walker to transfer. Listening to Walker, though, it wasn't just about being homesick. "I'm kind of homesick and I don't think I'm getting a pretty good deal up here. I think Coach Majors is a little prejudiced about playing me. He really didn't know what I could do until he started me in that one game [against Temple]. I've had it on my mind for some time but I just mentioned it to my brother. There is a very slim chance I'll be back here next year."[47] Walker had NFL aspirations, and there was a rumor he had signed with an agent, Pitt alum and Miami-based agent Anthony Pace. If true, it would negate his eligibility.

As the situation developed, it was found out that Pace also met with Morsillo, a meeting arranged by the athletic director at Midland High School. Morsillo met with him but declined to sign. Cas Myslinski was working with the NCAA to determine if Walker had violated any rules.

Even with the Walker situation, which also included his brother Leverga, Majors had to prepare for spring drills with eighty-four players returning.

All of a sudden, talk of Elliott transferring to Miami was gone. The concern now was whether he could play at all. The first ruling by the NCAA was not in the Walkers' favor, and it was thought they would be suspended. But when the school appealed the findings and the NCAA allowed both players to practice, Majors began to feel confident that they would be allowed to play in the fall.

Another off-field issue plagued Pitt in the spring. Tony Dorsett had amassed $1,145 in fines with ninety-nine unpaid parking. He had his car impounded until he came up with a down payment of $400 and then promised to pay $100 a month until they were paid off.

Majors was as frustrated with the off-the-field issues as he was with his team's performance the first few days of the drills, claiming that it was inexperience causing the problems. It got worse when Johnson was injured with a torn knee cartilage. Majors hoped that the damage wasn't as severe as he feared. Eventually, the offense was on track, as both Dorsett and Walker were playing in an impressive manner.

The most important aspect of the spring drills was the race for starting quarterback, which was close. Haygood had a slight advantage because he had more varsity experience, but Cavanaugh's strong arm was opening some eyes. The two would get an opportunity to shine, as the team was having its first big scrimmage of the year at Hershey. While fans were waiting to see the new version of the Panthers, Majors got some great news two days before the scrimmage when it was announced that the Walker brothers were eligible. While they were in violation by signing with Pace, it was decided that they had been misled by the attorney, and the contracts were voided.

The scrimmage took place on a windy day, so neither quarterback threw well, but Walker led the way with 171 yards while Haygood chipped in 127. Cavanaugh was more impressive through the air, with 150 yards on 11 completions; Haygood was only 3 for 11. It was also the first time Majors unleashed the veer, playing in the formation the entire contest. Cavanaugh and Dorsett, the latter of who ran for 131 yards, led the Blue to a 21–18 win over the Gold in front of 9,200 fans. Two weeks later, the teams met again in the annual Blue and Gold Game at Pitt Stadium.

With journalists Sam Nover and Pat Livingston coaching the teams, the veer looked impressive as the Blue once again won, 21–17. The two teams combined for 579 yards rushing; Dorsett, Hutton and Walker all eclipsed 100 yards. It had been a tougher spring than Majors imagined, but it was over, and he could look toward the fall and hope football was the only thing he had to focus on.

As fall practice began, Haygood was still at the top of the depth chart at quarterback. "It took two, three years to convince me to change to the veer. I wouldn't want a team without a quarterback who could run," Majors explained.[48] It didn't mean Haygood would have the job when the team opened the season against the Georgia Bulldogs, but it made sense in terms of where the competition was as the club began fall practice at the University of Pittsburgh–Johnstown campus. Before they left for UPJ, the team stopped at Pitt Stadium in uniform to meet the press and Panther fans alike. It was then off for the drive to their summer home, which usually involved a brutal, hot and humid experience for the players. There was another off-the-field moment as the team was about to head off for camp: coach Majors was named preseason Coach of the Year by *Playboy* magazine.

Dorsett reported to camp a little heavier, at 183 pounds, and was looking to improve on a disappointing 1974 campaign that saw his rushing total decreased from his freshman season, more than 500 yards less. Using the veer to emphasize his skill was expected to put him back in the Heisman talk.

On the defensive side, despite the talent that was returning, Pitt was coming off a disappointing season. And the loss of Burley, Kirby, Hyde, Daviston, Bulino and Hodge was going to be felt. Sherrill thought that his returning players and the young talent they had recruited over the previous few years would be enough to get the team back into shape.

The coaching staff was happy with the effort the team was giving, even though they felt the offense had quite a bit of work to do in the new offensive formation. Cavanaugh missed the first full scrimmage with a sore back. Haygood was effective, leading the running game out of the veer, although he was only 2 for 8 passing. When Cavanaugh returned, the passing game picked up, to Majors's approval.

Three freshmen impressed the staff with their play: Jones, Delaney and Mike Balzer. Steve Clemons and Joe Como decided to leave the team and end their Pitt careers before they had begun. It was a turnaround for Jones, who had been frustrated with the coaches for his lack of playing time in camp and had been running laps after practices because of his attitude. As the team broke camp at Johnstown, another player caught their attention. Junior Carson Long hit a 57-yard field goal that, with the wind, traveled a reported 70 yards. He was also successful from 48 yards into a strong wind.

The Panthers appeared to be ready for a third season under Majors, with a difficult schedule that included Georgia and Oklahoma to begin it and Notre Dame and Penn State to conclude the campaign. It would be a year that looked like the program was not moving forward, but a dominating upset sent the Panthers on the course for a national championship a year later.

GAME ONE

THE UNIVERSITY OF PITTSBURGH PANTHERS 19
THE UNIVERSITY OF GEORGIA BULLDOGS 9
SANFORD STADIUM, ATHENS, GEORGIA
SEPTEMBER 6, 1975
RECORD: 1-0-0

It was only two years earlier when the Johnny Majors era began with a stunning tie in Athens, Georgia, against Vince Dooley and the Bulldogs. He would begin his third season looking to introduce his veer offense in the same stadium. As in 1973, it was a difficult opponent to begin the season, but one the Panthers were prepared for.

Dooley also ran the veer at Georgia but had a more experienced quarterback in Matt Robinson. Robinson, as Cavanaugh would do a year later, gave the Bulldogs a QB who not only knew how to run the offense but also gave them the threat of the pass, as he led the SEC in 1973 with 22 yards per pass play. Robinson would also have the advantage of going against an inexperienced Pitt defense trying to rebound from a substandard season defending against the run. Pitt's veer offense had the advantage of debuting against the last-place defensive team in the SEC.

On top of a new offense and a young defense, Majors had the challenge of the new NCAA rule limiting traveling squads to forty-eight players. The Panther head coach was not only challenged by figuring out who his forty-eight-man team would be traveling to Georgia, but he was also irritated at the NCAA for instituting a rule that limited home teams to sixty players. Luckily for Majors, Paul "Bear" Bryant challenged the new rule in court and won. At least temporarily, this expanded the visiting team to sixty players again. The NCAA planned to appeal, but in the meantime, things would be a little easier for Johnny going to Athens.

Majors ended up bringing fifty-two players and took the field at Sanford Stadium in ninety-degree heat. Pitt had a difficult time moving the ball, and the Bulldogs dominated the first half. They stopped Dorsett for 17 yards in the first two quarters and ran through that Panther defense inside the 5-yard line on the first series. Pitt forced a fumble that Romano pounced on when the Bulldogs went for it on fourth-and-1. Moments later, Haygood, who held on to the starting quarterback position in the off-season, tossed an interception at the Pitt 25 that Georgia eventually converted into a touchdown to take a 7–0 lead.

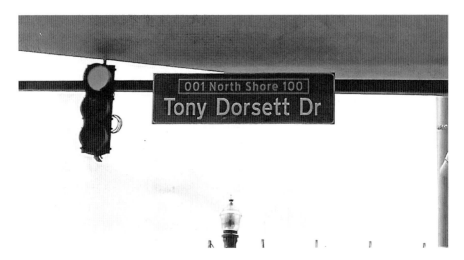

The record books run deep for Tony Dorsett, the only Heisman Trophy winner in school history. A member of both the Pro Football and the College Football Halls of Fame, Dorsett received another honor when Heinz Field and PNC Park were built. As part of an effort to honor some of the city's greatest sports legends, a street was named after Dorsett not far from Heinz Field. *Courtesy of David Finoli.*

In the second half, the veer finally got moving, but Pitt needed a turnover to get on the board. After the Panthers recovered a fumbled punt return on the Bulldog 27, Long converted on a 37-yard field goal to make it 7–3. Another fumble recovery, this one by Bob Jury, set up a 27-yarder by Long to cut the Georgia lead to 1 point.

Dorsett finally got untracked late in the third quarter. The junior halfback, who had 104 yards for the game, ran for 27 yards late in the third quarter to lead a drive that ended up with Walker bolting over from the 1 to give Pitt its first lead of the contest, 12–7, a score that remained after Haygood, who contributed 65 yards rushing, was stopped on the 2-point conversion.

After Panther punter Larry Swider took a safety rather than punt from his end zone and give Georgia great field position, the Pitt defense, which was magnificent in the second half and limited the Bulldogs to 278 total yards in the contest, stopped the home team once again and forced a punt. Dorsett once again was the main force of a game-ending drive with a 36-yard run that led to a Haygood 3-yard run that put the game away for the Panthers in an impressive 19–9 victory.

Once again, Majors frustrated Dooley and his Bulldogs. He would do it one more time a year later, when Pitt faced Georgia for the national championship in the Sugar Bowl.

Game Two

The University of Oklahoma Sooners 46
The University of Pittsburgh Panthers 10
Owen Field, Norman, Oklahoma
September 20, 1975
Record: 1-1-0

After an exciting victory at Georgia to open the 1975 campaign, Pitt would travel to Oklahoma to play the number-one team in the nation in the Associated Press poll for the first time since 1966. With a week off to prepare for the Sooners, Johnny Majors was looking forward to the opportunity to pit his new offense against the best team in the land.

To say Oklahoma was a powerhouse would be an understatement. They were coming off a decisive 62–7 win against Oregon. Since Barry Switzer, who used to be a defensive coach for Majors at Iowa State, had taken over, the Sooners were undefeated, with a 22-0-1 mark. A 7–7 tie against USC in 1973 was the only blemish for a team that won the Associated Press national championship in 1974.

The oddsmakers in Las Vegas made the fifteenth-ranked Panthers a 28-point underdog, not believing Majors's claim that Pitt was coming to Norman looking for a win. Running back Joe Washington had been every bit as spectacular for the Sooners as Dorsett had been for the Panthers and was challenging Steve Owens's career rushing mark for Oklahoma. Their defense at times also appeared to be impenetrable, as they limited the Oregon Ducks to 48 yards rushing on 33 attempts in their opener. While spectacular, Oklahoma was on a three-year probation for recruiting violations and was ineligible to appear on TV in 1975. In 1973, they had been allowed to be on TV but banned from playing in a bowl game. A year later, they were prohibited from TV and the postseason. This season, the TV ban was still in place, but the Sooners could finally play in a bowl game.

Sherrill knew it would be difficult to stop Oklahoma, so he hoped his defense could force turnovers, as it had against Southern Cal the year before. That had allowed them to stay close in a contest in which they had been dominated statistically. Unfortunately, it was Pitt that put the ball on the ground, losing 4 fumbles, 3 of which led to touchdowns, and they were never in this game.

By the end of the third quarter, the Panthers veer offense could muster only 65 yards as Oklahoma scored 23 unanswered points in the first half, going into the locker room with a 23–0 lead. While Long cut it to 23–3 with a 46-yard field goal, the Sooners put it away with 3 more touchdowns to extend their advantage to 44–3. Haygood made it 44–10 with Pitt's most impressive play of the contest, a 54-yard touchdown pass to Farmer. But Oklahoma scored the game's final points, blocking a Larry Swider punt in the end zone for a safety, making made the final score 46–10.

The pounding Pitt took was brutal. They allowed 378 yards rushing; Washington looked very much a Heisman candidate with 166 yards and 3 touchdowns. Walker was the only part of the veer that looked decent, with 63 yards on 13 carries. Dorsett had the worst game of his collegiate career: 17 yards on 11 attempts. Hutton and Haygood had 13 and -1 yards, respectively. While Oklahoma was focusing on the run, Haygood had some success through the air, completing 9 of 12 for 166 yards. But it wasn't nearly enough to make the game close. Once again, Pitt failed against a top-twenty team.

Fortunately, Pitt would open up the home portion of the season against William & Mary the next week before heading into the eastern part of their schedule. It would be a chance to get over this one-sided defeat and hopefully get their third season under Majors headed in the right direction.

Game Three

The University of Pittsburgh Panthers 47
The College of William & Mary Indians 0
Pitt Stadium
September 27, 1975
Record: 2-1-0

After a one-sided beating by the number-one team in the nation, Pitt finally returned to Pittsburgh for their home opener against the College of William & Mary, led by coach Jim Root and his staff, which included Lou Tepper, future Illinois head coach as well as at western Pennsylvania division II schools at Edinboro and IUP.

With so much speed and talent in the Pitt backfield, which seemingly made the veer a perfect offense for them, one had to feel sorry for the Indians. The frustration the Panthers felt the week before against Oklahoma most likely would be taken out against this undermanned Southern Conference squad.

Safety J.C. Wilson would miss the contest with strained knee ligaments, prompting Sherrill to put Jim Farkey in his spot. And a shoulder injury to Perko made him doubtful. Otherwise, Pitt was hungry, angry and a 28-point favorite.

What the 31,022 fans expected when they entered Pitt Stadium was a team eager to show off its new offense against a team that wasn't talented enough to contain it. While William & Mary's defense was surprisingly tough in the first half, limiting Dorsett to only 15 yards on his first 6 carries. Pitt's defense against the Indian version of the veer was incredible. Randy Cozens and Mike Balzer led the way, limiting the visitors to only 88 yards rushing.

The Panthers threatened five times in the first half but could only muster a lone touchdown—a 1-yard run by Dorsett, who twice came out of the contest with injuries in the first half—wrapped around a school-record 4 Carson Long field goals, to take a 19–0 lead at the end of the first half. Finally, in the second half, Majors got a chance to see just how dangerous his veer offense was.

It was impressive enough that the passing game was better than expected for the second week in a row, as Haygood completed 9 of 15 for 134 yards. Of these, 4 completions were to Gordon Jones in his Pitt Stadium debut. The majority of his catches were of the spectacular kind. But the rushing attack was the key to the win.

They ran for 386 yards as Pitt's Heisman hopeful finished with 142 yards. His backfield mate, Elliott Walker, had 105. Dorsett had touchdown runs of 33 and 5 yards, while Walker and Hutton also scored to lead the Panthers to an easy 47–0 win, their largest margin of victory since defeating Ohio Wesleyan, 59–0, during their last national championship campaign in 1937.

The matchup the next week at Pitt Stadium would be more difficult, as the Panthers were entertaining Duke. But for the time being, the offense got some confidence that they sorely needed.

Game Four

The University of Pittsburgh Panthers 14
The Duke University Blue Devils 0
Pitt Stadium
October 4, 1975
Record: 3-1-0

The veer offense had finally taken hold against William & Mary, but Johnny Majors knew that his team still had some space to improve, as they were taking on a tougher opponent in Duke the following week. "We're still a little slow on our take off, but it was better in the second half. We're close to having some real fine things to happen in our new offense."[49] He made sure he communicated to the press that he was committed to this offense, but he also claimed: "It is the technique and execution that are bogging us down at times. But I still believe the veer is best suited for our personnel."[50]

The Blue Devils were coming off their first victory of the season, a 26–11 defeat of Virginia, after losing their first two contests to USC and South Carolina. Head coach Mike McGee had an effective offense, but their leading running back, Art Gore, hurt his ankle in the victory over the Cavaliers and was not able to make the trip to Pittsburgh. Despite the injury, McGee felt that this was the best team at the school in the ten seasons and thought they'd give Pitt a competitive contest, despite being 13-point underdogs.

While Duke would be without an important piece of their offense, the Panthers would be without the speedy receiver Karl Farmer, who was out with a bruised knee.

There was an important moment outside of the contest that the 33,778 fans at Pitt Stadium enjoyed. They had a chance to celebrate Ave Daniell and Joe Skladany at halftime as the two Pitt greats were elected to the College Football Hall of Fame. Another interesting tidbit was that Pittsburgh Pirate pitcher Steve Blass, who would go on to iconic stature as the longest-tenured Pirate broadcaster in the history of the franchise, began his broadcasting career as the guest color man on the Duke football radio network.

On the field, it was the defense that turned out to be the stars of the game instead of the much-talked-about veer offense. The Panthers did run for 251 yards, led by Dorsett's 84 and Haygood's 80, but they only scored twice, once each by the two top rushers, for a 14–0 Pitt victory. In the game, Dorsett became the first Pitt back to break the 3,000-yard barrier.

Led by Randy Holloway, who had 2 sacks and 1 batted-down pass, Arnie Weatherington and Al Romano, Pitt extended its shutout streak to eight consecutive quarters. Despite allowing 191 yards through the air—a high under Majors to that point of his career at the school—the Panthers limited the Duke running attack to 33 yards. Weatherington stated that "this one was a little more satisfying than the shutout against William & Mary."[51] Romano had some fun with that Panther offense. "We figured they owe us one. The defense is one up after two shutouts."[52]

GAME FIVE

THE UNIVERSITY OF PITTSBURGH PANTHERS 55
THE TEMPLE UNIVERSITY OWLS 6
VETERANS STADIUM, PHILADELPHIA, PENNSYLVANIA
OCTOBER 11, 1975
RECORD: 4-1-0

In 1974, Temple coach Wayne Hardin was bragging about his team and the fact that they were close to being the second-best team in the East behind Penn State. Pitt did eventually quiet them with a 35–24 victory, but it was thought that they could still compete with the Panthers. A year later, Pitt was about to make a statement, as both the defense and the offense of Johnny Majors squad would show Hardin and his crew they still had a long way to go to be on the same level as Pitt.

After an embarrassing battle against top-ranked Oklahoma, the Pitt defense had become the stars of the team with back-to-back shutouts, the first time a Pitt defense had achieved that since 1945. They knew that continuing the streak against Temple would be difficult. Defensive back Larry Felton said: "We've got to improve our reading and Coach Sherrill says we've got to get meaner…a lot meaner. He's a nice guy off the field but when he's on it, he wants everyone to be mean and tough."[53] Defensive line coach Jim Dyar felt the defense learned a lot in the Oklahoma debacle. "We learned something from Oklahoma. Oklahoma was great that day because they were up. They were vicious hitters and they made our players conscious of what hitting can do."[54]

Offensively, the team wasn't where it wanted to be at this point, but they were still ahead of where they were a year earlier. Most notable, Dorsett was improved, although still not at his freshman level. His average per carry was up 1.2 yards per game, to 5.4, and he had less touches, so he would be more rested.

The Temple offense was led by quarterback Pat Carey, who transferred from Pitt three years before and was replacing superstar Steve Joachim. It had been a completely different 1975 campaign without Joachim. They were 1-3, coming off a win against Cincinnati, 21–17, and had been roundly defeated by WVU and Boston College after a fine effort on opening day, losing to Penn State, 26–25. The Owls struggled against Elliott Walker the year before when Dorsett was shelved with an injury, and now they would have to figure out a way to stop both players.

Coming into the contest, the Pitt offense was healthy, but the defense would be missing Bob Jury and Chuck Bonasorte with injuries. While they were important players to lose, in the end, it didn't matter. The Panthers had their biggest rout since they defeated Ohio Wesleyan, 59–0, in 1937, the second time in three weeks that the 1937 contest was mentioned. It was a thorough and complete beating of Hardin and his Owls.

It was a rainy day in Philadelphia as 10,731 were on hand at Veterans Stadium to witness the one-sided affair. Carey started the contest in an efficient manner, leading Temple downfield before Leroy Felder blocked a field goal. J.C. Wilson picked up the block and raced 52 yards to give Pitt a 7–0 lead. After stopping Temple, the Panthers got the ball on their own 25. Haygood stunned the Temple defense, which was prepared for the run, by lofting a bomb on the first play from scrimmage for a 75-yard touchdown pass to Gordon Jones.

Late in the first quarter, the Owls broke the Panther shutout streak with a field goal. After a Dorsett fumble in the second quarter, Wilson, who had an incredible game with the pickup of a blocked punt, 2 interceptions and 2 fumble recoveries, picked off a Carey pass. Dorsett would score twice, on a 51-yard reception and then on a 24-yard run, with a Walker 5-yard run sandwiched in between, to give the Panthers an insurmountable 35–3 lead at the half.

In the second half, Long hit 2 field goals to go along with a 6-yard interception return for a score by Wilson and a 14-yard pass from Cavanaugh to Steve Gaustad after Jeff Delaney picked off a pass to go along with his fumble recovery earlier in the half. The final was 55–6 in a contest in which Dorsett ran for 114 yards and added 80 more catching the ball. While the shutout streak ended, the defense had not allowed a touchdown in twelve. It was a complete win, one that put Majors over the .500 mark in his overall coaching career (41-40-2).

GAME SIX

THE UNIVERSITY OF PITTSBURGH PANTHERS 52
THE UNITED STATES MILITARY ACADEMY CADETS 20
MICHIE STADIUM, WEST POINT, NEW YORK
OCTOBER 18, 1975
RECORD: 5-1-0

With three wins in a row by a combined 116–6 margin, the Panthers were gaining confidence. They were now seventeenth in the UPI poll and were hoping this run of outstanding play would lift them back into the national rankings on a more consistent basis. Up next was a trip to West Point to play Homer Smith and the Army Cadets.

After winning their first two games of the season, the Cadets were going in the opposite direction of Pitt. They were in the midst of a three-game losing streak, the last two contests by a combined score of 88–24, to Stanford and Duke. They had one offensive player of note in quarterback Leamon Hall, who came into the contest ranked thirteenth in the nation in passing. Other than that, they were fairly thin on the offensive side of the ball.

The defense, which had given up only 6 points in the previous three games, was coming off a game in which they had several outstanding performances against Temple. Randy Cozens had an incredible contest, along with Weatherington, Cecil Johnson and J.C. Wilson, who had transferred from Tampa after the school dropped football. He was named to the UPI Backfield of the Week, having had 2 interceptions, 2 fumble recoveries and 2 touchdowns. He was the first defensive player to be selected for such an honor. The defensive group was looking forward to facing an undermanned Army squad. Smith also recognized the greatness of Pitt's defense. "The spirit of their defense is another concern—the whole backfield speed and on the line Romano doesn't get blocked and Cozens jumps over people to make tackles. It's the best defense we've had to face by far."[55]

Pitt was coming into this game fairly healthy. Ed Wilamoswki, Chuck Bonasorte, Steve Gaustad and Karl Farmer were the only ones questionable. Any thoughts of an upset of a confident club that was a 23-point favorite ended quickly. Once again, Pitt raced off to a dominant early lead. They went on an 80-yard drive on their first series, ending with a 6-yard touchdown run for a 7–0 lead, then doubled it following a Denny Moorhead interception at the Army 24-yard line that led to a Tony Dorsett 14-yard TD run.

Army cut the lead in half with a 23-yard scoring pass from Hall to Don Briggs. It was the first touchdown the Panther defense allowed since the Oklahoma contest, but Pitt quickly rose to the occasion with three more Dorsett touchdown runs in the first half, one from 66 yards and the other two from 21 and 35, to give the Panthers a 35–7 halftime lead. Despite losing a fumble in the second quarter, Dorsett was having a phenomenal day, with 217 yards rushing in the first half. The 4 touchdowns gave him 34 for his career, putting him ahead of Andy Hastings and George McLaren as the all-time Pitt touchdown career leader.

By all accounts, he could have easily eclipsed the 400-yard plateau had he played the whole contest, but Majors didn't let him play much in the second half, and Dorsett finished with a school-record 268 yards on only 21 carries, leaving him only 271 yards short of his third consecutive 1,000-yard season. Walker took control at that point with 107 yards and 1 touchdown that gave Pitt a 52–7 lead early in the final quarter. With the defense full of reserve players, Army scored the final two touchdowns of the contest to make the final 52–20.

For the Panthers it was a record-setting offensive performance, as they broke both the total offense mark for a single game with 610 yards and the single-game rushing record of 530. Both records had been set in a contest against Duke fifty-one years earlier, in 1924, when they had 577 total yards with 468 rushing. Scoring 107 points in two games and 168 over the four-game winning streak sent a message to other schools preparing to stop their now-potent offense.

As good as Pitt's veer had looked over the four-game win streak, Joe Paterno was trying to play head games with Majors following Penn State's 39–0 victory over West Virginia. "I don't think we have to worry about the veer anymore. We've seen it twice in a row and I think we've learned how to contain it."[56] He would show that they had a few weeks later at Three Rivers Stadium.

Game Seven

The Naval Academy Midshipmen 17
The University of Pittsburgh Panthers 0
Pitt Stadium
October 25, 1975
Record 5-2-0

Things were certainly going well for the University of Pittsburgh's football program. After a humbling defeat to the number-one team in the nation, they had reeled off four consecutive dominant wins and now were ranked in both polls. Pitt entered the Associated Press poll at number seventeen following a win at Army. While Army was considered a poor service-academy team, Navy had played well under George Welsh despite losing to Boston College the week before, 17–3. They were 4-2, with their only other loss being to Washington, 14–13. They had one of the best defensive teams in the country, which made for a bigger challenge to Pitt than Army had given them.

Tony Dorsett was coming off an incredible performance against Army, after which he was selected to the UPI Backfield of the Week and was the *Sports Illustrated* Offensive Player of the Week. But Welsh had a defensive team that was hell-bent on stopping him. Out of the veer, the Panther rushing offense was nineteenth in the country, scoring 32.8 points per game, sixth nationally. Navy had a defense led by Chet Moeller and defensive tackle Dave Papak, who was from Monongahela, that gave up only 104.7 yards rushing, eighth in the country, while allowing only 9.7 points per game, fifteenth best. The contrast made for an interesting contest, even though Pitt was installed as a 13-point favorite.

The excitement over Pitt's success had the bowl games excited. The Sun and Liberty Bowls were on hand at Pitt Stadium, and the Orange Bowl had the Panthers listed as one of its ten most-wanted programs for the major bowl. Still, with all the excitement, Majors knew that Welsh would have his team prepared, especially as Pitt would be without three key players: Farmer, Al Chesley and Bonasorte. Johnny knew Welsh's ability as a coach and that his defense was a true threat, and he was concerned. As the homecoming contest went on, it was apparent just how good Welsh's defense was.

The Navy defense couldn't stop Dorsett, as the junior running back ran for 122 yards, upping his career total to 3,441, seventh in college football history at that time. But Moeller, who was playing with a broken thumb, and his teammates stopped everyone else, limiting Pitt to a season-low 223 yards of total offense.

Four Panther turnovers and costly penalties also led to the upset. Early on, Gordon Jones returned a punt 52 yards before a fumble by Dorsett at the Navy 15 gave the Cadets the ball. They took advantage of the fumble, driving 85 yards to take a 7–0 advantage. The Panthers then seemingly tied the contest when the Heisman Trophy candidate broke through Navy for a 75-yard touchdown run. Unfortunately, an illegal-motion penalty negated the long run and kept the Cadets in the lead.

Navy began the second half with a 61-yard scoring drive to increase their advantage to 14–0. Pitt had a chance to cut it in half when Randy Holloway jumped on a fumble in the third quarter in Midshipmen territory, but the Navy defense held the veer offense of Pitt, and Carson Long then missed on a 46-yard field goal. A 40-yard fourth-quarter field goal following Elliott Walker's trick pass at the Navy 27 was picked off by Moeller and returned to the Pitt 29 made the score 17–0. A goal-line stand by Navy late in the game secured the first shutout on a Panther offense since Pitt's loss to Army, 26–0, in 1968.

While Majors tried to stay positive after the upset loss, he certainly had to be furious at his team's effort. It was a defeat that threatened the postseason possibility for Pitt.

Game Eight

The University of Pittsburgh Panthers 38
The Syracuse University Orangemen 0
Archbold Stadium, Syracuse, New York
November 1, 1975
Record: 6-2-0

In twenty-four hours, the University of Pittsburgh football program went from one of the most attractive teams in the eyes of bowl representatives, to a squad that wondered if it would get an opportunity to play in a postseason contest, following the 17–0 upset loss to Navy. With nationally ranked Notre Dame and Penn State at the end of Pitt's schedule, the games against Syracuse and West Virginia on their two-game road trip became must-wins if the program hoped for a bid.

The team they'd face this week was the Syracuse Orangemen at Archbold Stadium in Syracuse. In Coach Frank Maloney's second season, he had Syracuse playing much better football. After a 2-9 mark his initial year, the Orangemen came into this contest at 4-3, including great efforts in losses to Navy and Penn State. Bill Hurley, who became a talented quarterback for the team, was a freshman and a dangerous running threat for the team, although the offense overall was not very effective at this point, scoring 10 points or less in four of the seven games they had played.

Majors was very disappointed in the loss to Navy. "The loss put a slowdown in our program. Certainly at this point I don't think we had one more disappointing. I'm disappointed we couldn't come back. The posture reinforcement I was looking for didn't come. We didn't bounce back. When you get shut out, that's a bad thing."[57] The fans at Pitt Stadium were also upset at the loss, which irritated Haygood. "We don't have the best fans in the world. I could feel the booing, but I don't play for the fans."[58] Majors hoped that his players had a short memory and could rebound against Syracuse. If they did, they would be going into the contest perhaps without Haygood, who had suffered a hip injury in the game. Cavanaugh took most of the snaps in practice during the week, and Majors felt he was ready if needed and thought they wouldn't have to make any changes in the veer with him running the show.

As game time approached, Haygood still hadn't practiced, so Cavanaugh got his opportunity. Farmer was also still missing, as was J.C. Wilson, who had had such a tremendous performance a couple of weeks earlier. Dorsett was healthy but was focused on getting revenge for what he thought was a cheap shot the year before in the game against Syracuse that had sprained his ankle, causing him to miss the contest against Temple.

Maloney was confident though, claiming that he was a good coach and that his team was second in the East behind Penn State. Those thoughts quickly subsided as the focused Panthers dominated Syracuse from the outset on a cold, windy and rainy day in upstate New York.

Cavanaugh played well and gave Pitt a passing option. While he attempted only 9 passes, he completed 6 for 167 yards and 3 touchdowns. On the ground, Dorsett added 158 yards, eclipsing the 1,000-yard plateau for the third time, while Elliott Walker chipped in 93. After a first-quarter 10-yard touchdown run by Walker, Cavanaugh hit Corbett for an 8-yard scoring toss and Dorsett broke through for a 73-yard run, giving Pitt a 21-point halftime lead. Long hit a field goal in the third, increasing the advantage to 24–0 before Cavanaugh made it a rout in the final quarter with a touchdown pass to Corbett from 17 yards and an 80-yard bomb to Jones. The 38–0 Pittsburgh victory showed Maloney that Syracuse was far from the second-best team in the East. The final Panther touchdown irritated the Syracuse coach, who felt Majors was trying to run up the score.

The win was thorough. Pittsburgh outgained the Orangemen, 429–175, and put their postseason ambitions back in play. Next up was their rival from West Virginia. It was to be a regional TV broadcast by ABC, as both programs were in the battle for the Lambert Trophy.

Game Nine

The West Virginia University Mountaineers 17
The University of Pittsburgh Panthers 14
Mountaineer Field, Morgantown, West Virginia
November 8, 1975
Record: 6-3-0

In the previous two seasons, when Pitt's season looked to be at a crossroads, a dominant victory over their rivals from Morgantown pushed them in the direction for a successful season. In 1975, in order to continue to push the program forward, Pitt needed once again to emerge victorious against the Mountaineers. Their postseason hopes seemed to be hanging on this contest, especially with two top-ten teams coming to Pittsburgh to end the Panthers' season and the Panthers' 0-7 mark under Majors against Associated Press top-twenty teams.

It wouldn't appear to be as easy a venture to beat the Mountaineers this year as it had been the previous two seasons. Coach Bobby Bowden had West Virginia headed in the right direction, coming into the game with a 6-2 mark and coming off two straight wins, against Virginia Tech and Kent State. They had a tough if unspectacular defense and were led offensively by running back Artie Owens, who would end up with 1,055 yards and a 6.6-yards-per-carry average while becoming the school's career rushing leader, and quarterback Dan Kendra.

The Panthers were coming off a one-sided win at Syracuse that vaulted them back into the Associated Press top twenty, at number twenty. Because it was now an attractive matchup, ABC decided to put the game on regional TV, which gave both schools a $170,000 payday. ABC was so thrilled with the contest that it sent its number-one broadcast team, Keith Jackson and Bud Wilkerson, to cover the game. It was the Panthers' first appearance on a regionally televised ABC contest in ten years. With Cavanaugh playing so well the week before, there was questions about whether Haygood would get his starting spot back if he was healthy. Bowden was convinced it would be Cavanaugh and prepared his team for that.

While it seemed that Haygood's hip was improving, Farmer's and Wilson's injuries were not, as both were listed as doubtful for the contest. As it turned out, Bowden, who was celebrating his forty-sixth birthday, was correct; Majors decided to start Cavanaugh.

The Panthers came into the contest as a touchdown favorite, but after a scoreless first half, it seemed to be a day when the veer offense for both teams would be sluggish. In the third quarter, WVU finally put points on the board to take a 7–0 lead. Pitt tied it up when Cavanaugh found Jones for a 28-yard score, but Owens had an exciting 23-yard TD run to put them back ahead, 14–7. The Pitt quarterback tossed his second scoring pass, this one to Dorsett from 9 yards to tie it at 14. Dorsett had been out of the contest for part of the fourth quarter after suffering an injury.

After being outplayed for most of the game, the Panthers finally looked like they would pull out the win they were desperate for when Dorsett, who had run for 112 yards in the game, rambled 22 yards deep into WVU territory to hopefully set up a Carson Long game-winning field goal. But a clipping penalty on the play moved the ball back to the 49. Cavanaugh then threw his second interception of the game. Led by Kendra, the Mountaineers moved down the field to the Pitt 17, but they fumbled, and Perko picked it up. It was late in the contest, and the game seemed headed to a tie.

An unsportsmanlike penalty was called against Joe Avezzano, who walked on the field trying to get Cavanaugh's attention. The quarterback lost track of downs and was trying to call a play on fourth down instead of punting. The error pinned the Panthers deep in their territory. Swider then punted to the Mountaineer 48 with eighteen seconds left. Kendra hit Randy Swinson with a 26-yard completion to the 22. With four seconds left, Bill McKenzie, an unrecruited kicker who made the team after waking on to a practice, hit a 38-yard field goal for the upset 17–14 victory.

As the sellout crowd spilled onto the field, Pitt's bowl hopes seemed to be over. With their two toughest games of the season left, the possibility was real that the Panthers would finish at 6-5. That would be a devastating blow to a program that was hoping to use 1975 as a step to the upper echelon of college football. To negate that prospect, they would have to finally defeat a top-twenty team in one of their final two games.

GAME TEN

THE UNIVERSITY OF PITTSBURGH PANTHERS 34
THE UNIVERSITY OF NOTRE DAME FIGHTING IRISH 20
PITT STADIUM
NOVEMBER 15, 1975
RECORD 7-3-0

When a young team finally figures out how to compete for championships, it's usually the result of a slow process that comes with time. It's not always easy to point to a specific point when it happened. For Johnny Majors Pitt Panthers, it was easy to point out that time. It happened just when it seemed a foregone conclusion that the team was about to fall back to mediocrity following a crushing loss to WVU. The date was November 15,

1975, when the ninth-ranked Notre Dame Fighting Irish came to town expecting to add another victory over Pitt. It turned out to be the day when Tony Dorsett went from a talented running back to a Panther icon and Pitt went from a good team to one that finally figured out how to become an elite program. It was perhaps the most important victory in modern Panther football history.

Once again, Majors had a tough decision to make at quarterback with Haygood now healthy. He was warming up in the third quarter of the WVU game, but the coach decided to let Cavanaugh continue. Notre Dame's sophomore quarterback, future NFL icon Joe Montana, who was from nearby Ringgold High School, had been effective in relief of starting quarterback Rick Slager, but a broken index finger put him on the sidelines for the contest.

Notre Dame wasn't having a tremendous campaign under first-year coach Dan Devine when compared to the ones that had been turned in by his predecessor, Ara Parseghian. The Irish came into the game with a 7-2 mark, losing to Michigan State and USC, but were ranked ninth in the nation and were coming off victories over Navy and Georgia Tech, the latter being the famed Rudy game that inspired the movie of the same name.

The Irish offense was inconsistent, but a defensive front that included Ross Browner, Steve Niehaus, Bob Golic, Willie Fry and Jeff Weston was strong enough to halt the veer offense of Pitt.

Pitt was perhaps as healthy as they had been all season. Wilson was ready to come back after missing two games with an injured ankle, as was Farmer, whose ankle was also feeling much better. But Pitt was still winless in three years against Associated Press top-twenty teams, and there was no reason to believe they would break that streak against Notre Dame. For the Irish, along with Montana's injury, their second-leading runner, Al Hunter, injured his hip and didn't make the trip to Pittsburgh

A bowl game seemed like a remote option for the Panthers after losing two of its last three games and the real possibility that they would be 6-5 after facing two top-ten opponents to close out the season. Representatives from the Sun Bowl were on hand at Pitt Stadium to see the home team; the Cotton and Sugar Bowls were there to see Notre Dame.

It was anticipated that this would be a down day for the Pittsburgh program, but as the Panthers soon found out, it was a game that showed everyone this team had the talent to compete for a national championship.

Majors decided to start Cavanaugh for the third straight game, but with Dorsett in the backfield, it really didn't matter who was behind center. On the first drive of the game, Dorsett ran for 57 yards, setting up a 3-yard TD run by Cavanaugh to give Pitt an early 7–0 lead. Notre Dame scored 10 unanswered points to go in front, 10–7, but a 71-yard run by the All-American halfback put the Panthers on top for good, 14–10.

Notre Dame made it a game, coming within 1 point after a field goal, but then the Panthers took control. After the Irish defense knocked the wind out of Dorsett, Walker came in for a 31-yard run that set up a Carson Long 42-yard field goal, then Dorsett returned to catch a pass from Cavanaugh then ran the remainder of the way for a 49-yard touchdown pass that gave him a school-record 14 touchdowns on the season and Pitt a 24–13 advantage in a half that saw Tony ramble for 161 yards and Walker accumulate 51 yards on only 4 attempts.

In the second half, Jones returned a punt 78 yards to set up another Long 3-pointer before Slager took Notre Dame on a 77-yard drive to cut the Panther lead to 7. As dominant as Pitt was, the ninth-ranked Irish were now within a touchdown. In the final quarter, Cavanaugh put all hopes for an Irish comeback away with a 1-yard TD run that gave the Panthers a 34–20 lead.

For Dorsett, it was a day of redemption. One of his dreams in high school was to go to Notre Dame, but an Irish scout thought he was too small and told the school his legs were too skinny and not to recruit him. He continued to rub it in that the scout was incorrect. After a 9-yard run late in the game after Majors put him back in when he realized he was near 300 yards rushing, Dorsett finished with 303 yards, still the only player in school history to eclipse the 300-yard plateau.

The victory was complete, as the team ran for 411 yards against the number-nine team in the nation and outgained them, 505–307. With the victory, Pitt got something else it didn't expect: a bid to the Sun Bowl to play either Kansas, Cal, UCLA, Stanford, Missouri, Arkansas or Texas A&M. Pitt would be only the second independent in the forty-year history of the bowl to receive a bid and would put on one heck of a show.

In the upcoming games against Penn State and Kansas, who eventually received the other Sun Bowl bid, Pitt would show that the performance against Notre Dame was the beginning of a new championship era at the school.

GAME ELEVEN

THE PENN STATE UNIVERSITY NITTANY LIONS 7
THE UNIVERSITY OF PITTSBURGH PANTHERS 6
THREE RIVERS STADIUM
NOVEMBER 22, 1974
RECORD: 7-4-0

With their biggest win in the Johnny Majors era to that point and a bid to the Sun Bowl in hand, the Pitt Panthers turned to the other albatross that had been hanging around their necks since 1966: Joe Paterno and the Penn State Nittany Lions. They had lost to Paterno in each of his first eight seasons at the helm of the Lions, the closest contest being a 14-point loss in 1969.

Paterno took great pleasure in taking jabs at his cross-state rivals over the years, especially at Majors. He made a comment about a young coach who recruited in an unethical manner during an interview for *Sports Illustrated* two years earlier that seemed to be referring to Majors. Earlier in the year, after Paterno's team defeated two schools that ran the veer offense, he exclaimed that his defense had solved the veer.

While Paterno usually solved any issue Pitt could cause his team, this seemed to be Pitt's best squad since 1963. They were once again ranked, coming in at seventeen in the Associated Press poll after the upset win against Notre Dame. They figured to give Paterno his toughest challenge in the series as the two teams met for the second straight season at Three Rivers Stadium in front of not only a sellout crowd but also a national TV audience on ABC.

Pitt was now confident it could finally move past Penn State, even though the Nittany Lions were ranked tenth. They were 8-2 and coming off a 15–14 upset loss to North Carolina State. They also struggled in victories against Temple, Kentucky and Maryland. Offensively, Penn State had no stars. John Andress was unspectacular at quarterback, and the team had a crew of undistinguished running backs, led by Woody Petchel and Duane Taylor. Defensively, it was another story, as the Nittany Lions gave up only 10.2 points per game, ninth in the country. They had a quick front defensive line that wasn't particularly physical, led by Ron Crosby. With the speed, it seemed feasible that Paterno actually had figured out how to stop the veer. Despite that, he was still impressed with how the Panthers defeated Notre Dame. "Their quickness. They're quicker than we've seen down there in a long time. It's the best Pitt team I've seen since 1963."[59]

Pictured here is Three Rivers Stadium. Built in 1970, it is better known as the home of the Pittsburgh Pirates and Pittsburgh Steelers. But in 1974 it housed one of the great rivalries in college football: Pitt versus Penn State. Having not defeated a Penn State team since 1965 and being routed in each game, Pitt played well before falling in the fourth quarter and losing 31–10 in 1974. They outplayed the Lions a year later but still lost, 7–6. *Courtesy of the University of Pittsburgh Athletics.*

As the game developed in front of 46,846 fans, it turned out that the legendary Penn State coach was right. The Panthers were healthy. Farmer was back in the lineup. Only Bonasorte, who spent much of the season injured, was out. It was a brutal defensive effort that Pitt appeared to win on several occasions. They broke a scoreless tie in the second quarter when Walker rambled for 37 yards, giving the Panthers a 6–0 lead. Long's extra point was blocked, and the Panthers held that advantage through the first three quarters.

The Panthers, who outgained the Nittany Lions on the evening, 300–241, made their lone defensive mistake in the final quarter when Chuck Fusina, who was replacing the ineffective Andress, hit Steve Geiss with a 28-yard touchdown toss to give Penn State a 1-point lead. It was at that point that Pitt began showing who the better team was on this evening. They drove to the Lions' 34 before Long's 51-yard attempt fell short. With 3:49 remaining in the ball game, Matt Cavanaugh scrambled before finding Gordon Jones with a 28-yard completion to the Lion 6. Pitt couldn't move any farther, and Long lined up for what appeared to be an easy 23-yard 3-point attempt. It sailed wide right and kept Penn State in front. Finally, the Panthers got the ball once again and, on the strength of a pass-interference call and a catch by Farmer at the 25, Pitt had one last chance to win the game with nine seconds left. Unfortunately, Long missed his third field goal of the contest as it fell short, giving Penn State the win.

Missing 3 field goals that he normally would have made devastated the strong-legged kicker. "What a horrible thing. I had everything lined up. The snaps were good and the holds were good. There was no excuse for it."[60]

While it was a disappointing loss, Pitt finally proved it could play with anyone in the nation. Luckily, Long rebounded in 1976, as would his teammates, who had turned the corner and could see competing for a national championship in front of them.

Chapter 7

1975 SUN BOWL

BLUEPRINT FOR A TITLE

*I*t was an exciting month for Pitt Panther football. They would have the opportunity to play in the Sun Bowl against another up-and-coming program, the Kansas Jayhawks. There would be many decisions for Johnny Majors to make before the contest, the main one being who the starting quarterback would be: Matt Cavanaugh, who played most of the last quarter of the season after Robert Haygood was injured; or Haygood, who was now fully healthy. Cavanaugh was a solid runner who had a better arm, while Haygood was much faster and gave the team a superior option on the run in the veer offense. It would have been nice if the Pitt coaches had nothing more than positional decisions to make before the most important bowl the program played since the 1955 Sugar Bowl, but that wasn't the case. Five of their players had legal issues coming into this contest that threatened to disrupt the momentum the team had gained since upsetting Notre Dame, 34–20.

The five players were facing grand jury indictments that could have meant jail sentences if they were indicted and then convicted in criminal court. There were two separate situations. Steven Pritchard and Al Chesley were arrested for presumably illegally charging students for long-distance telephone calls. This came on the heels of an accusation of stealing a tape recorder valued at $235 from a car in a campus parking garage. Chesley also had twenty-two outstanding parking tickets valued at $190. The second situation involved Perko, John Pelusi and David Treiber, who were charged with the assault of Robert Carney and his girlfriend outside of a campus bar.

Robert Haygood began the 1976 season as the Panther starting quarterback following his phenomenal performance in the 1975 Sun Bowl, where he ran for 101 yards to capture the MVP for the contest. Unfortunately, his career ended against Georgia Tech in the second game of the season when he tore ligaments in his knee. *Courtesy of the University of Pittsburgh Athletics.*

The university was concerned about both situations, but it was irritated with how the latter was being reported. It was their opinion that Perko, Pelusi and Treiber had been enticed into the fight by Carney after the three players were invited to the front of the line waiting to get into the bar after the win over the Irish. Carney was upset at the situation, and it was at this point that the university believed the fight started. Because the school believed the three did not start the fight, it thought that they would not be suspended against the Jayhawks. The situation with Pritchard, who played little and didn't even have a number assigned to him, and Chesley was not as clear. Their opportunity to play in the Sun Bowl was in jeopardy.

The two situations came on the heels of Dorsett being brought to court over $1,145 worth of parking tickets earlier in the year, and the case of two unnamed juniors who were arrested in October for impersonating the police and trying to intimidate gay individuals. Dorsett's case was settled; the one against the two juniors was dropped due to lack of evidence.

It was hoped that the off-the-field incidents weren't taking the Panthers' minds off the task at hand: defeating a very good Kansas squad with quarterback Norman Cromwell at the helm. Cromwell, who later became a three-time All-Pro safety with the Los Angeles Rams, wasn't much of a threat as a passing quarterback. But he was dangerous running the football, leading the running attack for the Jayhawks with 1,223 yards. For his efforts, he was named the Big Eight Offensive Player of the Year. In his backfield he had future Pittsburgh Steeler Laverne Smith, who contributed 982 yards for an average of 6.9 yards per carry.

Cromwell began his career with Kansas as a safety, leading the defensive backs with 85 tackles while pulling in 3 interceptions. After hiring Alabama offensive coordinator Robert "Bud" Moore before the 1975 campaign, the Kansas coach decided that Cromwell would make a great option quarterback. His intuition proved correct. The Jayhawks went from 4-7 in 1974 to 7-4, a season that saw them defeat the eventual national champion Oklahoma Sooners, 23–3. That was the same Sooner team that destroyed Pitt in the second game of the season. Kansas finished fourth in the Big Eight and were ranked nineteenth in the country by the end of the season.

Going against his third top-twenty team in a row in Pitt's second bowl game in three seasons provided Majors with a chance to reflect. "Truthfully I can't say I expected to be in two bowl games in three years. With Pitt's schedule I figured we'd do well if we won 40% of our games by this time."[61]

If a .400 winning percentage was all Majors expected, he must have been extremely proud coming to El Paso for this Sun Bowl matchup. Bowl officials also had to be proud of their decision to invite the Panthers immediately after their Notre Dame victory. Featuring an exciting back like Tony Dorsett, the Sun Bowl had its first sellout in the forty-one-year history of the game.

Two exciting teams would be on the field. Majors explained that both Cavanaugh and Haygood would play in the contest. As the game went on, it was apparent that Haygood was going to be the main performer. With Walker and Dorsett running out of the veer, the team that beat Oklahoma during the regular season looked relatively helpless defensively against the Panthers.

The weather had been difficult during the week in El Paso. Sleet fell at times, but the Panthers were focused and practiced well, even though they had heard the unfortunate news that their defensive coordinator, Jackie Sherrill, was leaving the school to take the head coaching job at Washington State. It was a deserved promotion for Sherrill, who had made the defensive unit at Pitt one of the toughest in the nation. The team was inspired to give him a good going-away gift with a bowl victory.

Pitt came into this game with a poor bowl record. Other than a 21–0 victory in the 1937 Rose Bowl, they had lost the rest, most by a significant margin. They were 1-6 in postseason games.

The trio of Walker, Dorsett and Haygood started off aggressive after the defense held Kansas on a fourth-and-1 at the Pitt 16. The Panther All-American went for 17 yards before Walker dashed all the way to the end zone on a 60-yard run for a 7–0 lead. Two short touchdown runs from Dorsett, one from 8 yards out and the other from 2, gave Pitt a dominant 19–0 lead at the end of the first half.

In the second half, Kansas played better, scoring on a 55-yard run by Smith to cut the Pitt lead to 19–7 at the end of the third. The fourth quarter was a back-and-forth tussle, with Walker scoring his second touchdown of the game on a 2-yard run, extending the Panther advantage to 26–7. Smith scored again on a 17-yard run, making it 26–13. Jones then snagged a 7-yard touchdown catch to restore Pitt's 19-point advantage. Kansas added a late touchdown to make the final score respectable, 33–19.

The defense struggled for the first time since the Oklahoma contest, allowing 342 yards rushing, but it made many important stops on third and fourth downs to keep the Jayhawk offense at bay. Pitt's veer was dynamic with Haygood at the controls. Dorsett ran for 142 yards on 17 carries and Walker had 123 yards on 11 carries. The game's MVP, Haygood, had 104 yards running and 60 yards passing.

It was a blueprint for competing for a national championship in 1976, which was something that made Majors nervous. "We'll be rated high in

1976 and there is not much I can do about it."[62] For now, the Panthers were fifteenth in the nation in the Associated Press poll and thirteenth in the UPI while winning eight games for the first time since the school went 9-1 in 1963.

Yes, the expectations were high. But, luckily, this was now a team that could handle high expectations.

Chapter 8

1976

PERFECTION

12-0-0

For three years, Panther coach Johnny Majors fought hard to diminish the expectations people had for his team. After victories over nationally ranked Notre Dame and Kansas and a close loss to tenth-ranked Penn State—a contest in which Pitt outplayed the Nittany Lions for the majority of the game—expectations were high as Majors began his fourth season. No longer were seven or eight wins enough. It was about competing for the national championship.

Street & Smith's 1976 football preview had them ranked twelfth nationally and first in the East, claiming that "with some luck and freedom from injuries, this could be the best Panther machine since the glory days of Jock Sutherland."[63] It got even worse for Majors when one of the most accurate preseason magazines of the day, *Gameplan Football Preview*, had the Panthers second behind only Michigan.

There were eighteen starters returning, including the entire backfield of Tony Dorsett, Elliott Walker and both quarterbacks, Robert Haygood and Matt Cavanaugh. Dorsett finished the 1975 campaign with 1,676 yards, while Walker had 903. Haygood got the start in the Sun Bowl and rambled for 101 yards. In front of them was a stellar offensive line that included John Hanhauser, Matt Carroll, John Pelusi, Tom Brzoza and Joe Stone. Tight end Jim Corbett and receivers Gordon Jones and Willie Taylor rounded out one of the top offensive units in the country.

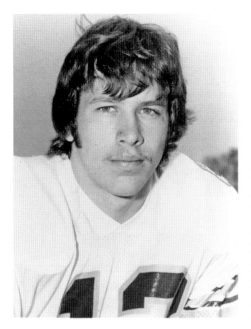

Tom Yewcic was ninth on the depth chart at quarterback to begin the season. He didn't have a uniform number, nor was he offered a scholarship. When both Robert Haygood and Matt Cavanaugh were injured, the fate of the 1976 national championship fell on his shoulders. He threw for 218 yards and ran for 116 more as he surprisingly led the Panthers to three consecutive victories before Cavanaugh's return against Army. *Courtesy of the University of Pittsburgh Athletics.*

While they struggled against Kansas, defensively, Pitt was vastly improved in 1975. The 1976 version was expected to be even better, with a defensive line of Cecil Johnson, Don Parrish, Al Romano, Randy Holloway and Dorsett's high school teammate Ed Wilamowski. At linebacker were Jim Cramer and Al Chesley. Jeff Delaney, Bob Jury, Leroy Felder and J.C. Wilson made for a premier defensive backfield.

The talented team was enhanced with another top recruiting class by the Pitt staff, including Willie Collier, Steve Fedell, Jo Jo Heath, Fred Jacobs, Larry Sims, Kurt Brechbill and Jeff Pelusi.

Perhaps the one fact that should have had Majors nervous was that his two coordinators had left in the off-season. After three years of staff stability, defensive coordinator Jackie Sherrill left to take over as the head coach of Washington State, and offensive coordinator George Haffner joined former WVU head coach Bobby Bowden, who became the new head man at Florida State, a job that Majors was rumored for. Sherrill took receivers coach Bob Leahy and graduate assistant Dave Campo with him. Johnny promoted his secondary coach, Joe Madden, to assistant head coach along with his former duties. Offensive line coach Joe Avezzano added offensive coordinator to his title, while Majors's defensive end coach Bobby Roper became the new defensive coordinator. Majors then hired Bill Cox as his quarterback and receiver coach, coming from Rice, where he was the offensive coordinator.

With the prospects of a memorable season in front of him, rumors of potential new jobs for Majors were becoming plentiful. Along with the Florida State rumor came one at Southern Methodist University (SMU), plus a job in the NFL as head coach of the New York Jets, all of which Majors said he wasn't interested in.

With Majors commitment to Pitt seemingly clear, spring drills began. The main competition once again was at quarterback, where both Haygood and Cavanaugh enjoyed success in 1975. Haygood was the better runner, which he exhibited clearly in the Sun Bowl, while Matt had potentially better passing skills, something the Panther head coach wanted to improve on in 1976. "A good passing attack comes in handy when you have to throw the ball. There will be big games when you have to throw to win. We've got to get the passing game ingrained into our philosophy in the spring," Majors felt.[64]

As the team began practice, they were able to put an end to the off-the-field issues that had plagued them the year before. Attorney Anthony Pace, who almost had the Walker brothers declared ineligible for signing them to a contract to be their agent when they became eligible, was sentenced to sixty days in jail and fined $500 with the threat of being disbarred. As far as the charges for illegally charging phone calls to a fellow student by Al Chesley and teammate Steve Pritchard, they were dropped after an out-of-court settlement, as were the charges of stealing stereo equipment, which they were acquitted of in mid-April. Three players, including Tom Perko, were acquitted of charges for a fight outside an Oakland bar.

The legal troubles were behind them, but Pitt was not sharp in spring practice. The favorite for the 1976 Heisman Trophy, Tony Dorsett, was sidelined with a pulled thigh muscle and later on hurt his ankle. Eventually, the team's performance began to improve, with Walker showing his skills in Dorsett's absence, especially in the Blue and Gold Game, where he ran for 100 yards and 4 touchdowns in the 27–16 victory for the Gold.

When the fall came, the excitement reached a new level. Sports information director Dean Billick and Majors went on an intense campaign to push Dorsett as the one and only Heisman candidate. While his historic numbers in 1976 were the ultimate reason he became the school's lone Heisman winner, Billick's and Majors efforts helped and became stories in the local Pittsburgh paper on almost a daily basis.

As Dorsett was being established as the leading preseason Heisman candidate, the team was starting to garner even more impressive honors, especially from the ones who would count the most as the season unfolded.

The Associated Press put them in the top ten to begin the season, at number nine. To help get more recognition, Pitt agreed to move its annual rivalry game against Notre Dame to the opening contest of the season, instead of near the end of it. The Fighting Irish were ranked eleventh and were hosting the Panthers on a regional ABC game. What hopes Pitt had in completing this incredible journey, from one of the worst teams in the country only four years earlier to a potential national championship contender, began in South Bend.

GAME ONE

THE UNIVERSITY OF PITTSBURGH PANTHERS 31
THE UNIVERSITY OF NOTRE DAME FIGHTING IRISH 10
NOTRE DAME STADIUM, SOUTH BEND, INDIANA
SEPTEMBER 11, 1976
RECORD: 1-0-0

In a season that began with such hope and enthusiasm, the opening week of the 1976 college football season for the University of Pittsburgh Panthers began to tell the tale of what kind of campaign it would be. They traveled to Notre Dame Stadium to play their rivals, and the home team had their eyes focused on revenge. Notre Dame defensive lineman Willie Fry exclaimed, "We don't have a particular fondness for Pitt in view of what they did to us last year."[65]

The year before, Pitt pulled off an exciting 34–20 upset over Notre Dame in a game that saw Tony Dorsett become the first—and to date only—Pitt running back to eclipse the 300-yard plateau, with 303 yards. The defense for the eleventh-ranked Irish was focused on him, to the point that the school reportedly let the grass on the gridiron grow a little higher in an effort to slow him down. Majors took a look at the field when the teams arrived at South Bend and stated: "It's the only place where I've ever seen a blade of grass blowing in the wind. It's higher than any grass I've seen at a stadium."[66] By game's end, the Irish found out that you can't slow greatness.

Notre Dame coach Dan Devine had been horrified to watch what the All-American did to his defense in 1975. "I've never been so embarrassed in my life. It's been my history to hold the big gun of the other team down, but we couldn't stop Dorsett. It was as fine a performance as I've seen in 28 years of coaching. We tried to make normal adjustments, but one guy kind of made

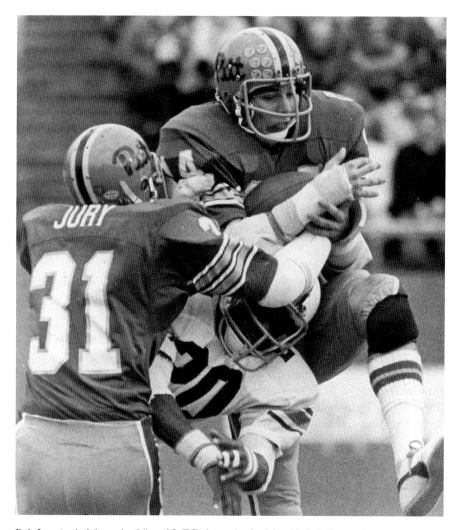

Bob Jury (*to the left, number 31*) and Jeff Delaney (*to the right with the ball*) were important parts of a great defensive backfield for the Panthers in 1976 that finished second in the nation with 28 interceptions. Delaney had 7 of them, while Jury was second in the nation with 10, which as of 2020 remains a Pitt record. Jury was named a consensus First Team All-American in 1977 and finished his career with a school-record 21 interceptions, still a Pitt mark as of 2020. *Courtesy of the University of Pittsburgh Athletics.*

them inadequate."[67] He also promised an Irish booster group that Dorsett would not run for 300 yards again, with Pitt boasting so much talent coming into the year he wouldn't have to for Pitt to win.

Dorsett came into the game healthy, but the week before the contest saw several Panthers injured. Walker, Gordon Jones and Hutton all had bad ankles, while Stone and Brzoza sat out practice with sore shoulders and Romano had a bad thigh. It was hoped that none of the injuries were serious, but fans wouldn't find out until game day. Majors put a gag order on his team, not allowing his players to be interviewed before the contest. As it turned out, Walker's injury was the most serious; he was still questionable as game time approached.

Even with all the excitement that surrounded Pitt and the fact that they were rated highly, they came into the contest a 3½-point underdog against the home team. As the game began, the capacity crowd of 59,035 thought they were going to see the revenge they had wanted for so long. Notre Dame ran down the field on the tough Pitt defense for an 86-yard drive to go ahead, 7–0. On Pitt's first series, they gave the ball to Dorsett, and he immediately set a tone, showing that high grass couldn't stop an icon. He ran 61 yards on his first carry, to the Irish 23. After a 19-yard completion to Corbett from Haygood, who got the starting nod at quarterback, Tony scored from 5 yards out to tie the game. Defensive back Leroy Felder then picked off a Rick Slager pass, returning it 35 yards to the 2, where Haygood burst into the end zone from 1 yard out as the home crowd quickly went from euphoric to quiet. Pitt was now on top, 14–7.

Jeff Delaney then picked off a pass of his own at the Irish 33. After two runs by Dorsett for 21 yards, Haygood went over again from the 1 to give the visitors a 2-touchdown lead. Jones then fumbled a punt, giving Notre Dame excellent field position, but they were unable to take advantage, as the Irish missed a field goal. Dave Reeve made up for it with a school-record 53-yard kick to cut the lead to 21–10. With Pitt driving late in the half and trying to put the game out of reach, Dorsett fumbled through the end zone to keep the score 21–10 at the half.

The Irish were determined in the second half and moved into Pitt territory on their first drive, but they fumbled at the Pitt 44, with Arnie Weatherington picking it up to stop their momentum.

Notre Dame's defense had succeeded in holding the Panther offense to negative rushing yards in the third quarter, but when Matt Cavanaugh came into the contest in the fourth, he put away any hopes of an Irish comeback. First, Pitt moved the ball, setting up a Carson Long field goal to make the score 24–10. After a bad Irish punt, Cavanaugh once again led the Panthers downfield, culminating in an 8-yard touchdown run by the junior quarterback to make the score 31–10, where it ended.

It was a statement game for Pitt and one in which Devine was correct. Dorsett didn't run for 300 yards—he only had 181. But it was enough to give Pitt the dominant victory over a top-twenty team—a team that hadn't lost an opener in thirteen years and only three times in the twentieth century. It was also a victory that catapulted the Panthers into the national championship race as they moved up to third in the Associated Press poll.

GAME TWO

UNIVERSITY OF PITTSBURGH PANTHERS 42
THE GEORGIA INSTITUTE OF TECHNOLOGY YELLOW JACKETS 14
GRANT FIELD, ATLANTA, GEORGIA
SEPTEMBER 18, 1976
RECORD: 2-0-0

It was a dream opening to the 1976 season. A dominant victory over a ranked team on the road. The win pushed Pitt to third in the nation in the Associated Press poll and fourth by United Press International. Majors hoped they could stay focused on their next opponent, the Georgia Tech Yellow Jackets. Georgia Tech was a small, quick team that could cause the Panthers issues, despite coming off a 27–17 loss to South Carolina.

The Panthers didn't come through the Notre Dame game unscathed, though. Joe Stone broke his jaw and receiver Randy Reutershan broke his foot. Reutershan didn't play, but the team was attempting to fit Stone with a specially made helmet to protect his jaw.

The Georgia Tech defense and coach, Pepper Rodgers, were looking for ways to stop the Panther All-American running back, Tony Dorsett, who had several impressive records in his sight. He was within 4 points of Andy Hastings's Pitt scoring records. He also needed to average only 86 yards per game to eclipse Archie Griffin's NCAA record of 5,177 yards that wasn't even a year old. It would be an advantage to play on the artificial turf of Grant Field, where Dorsett's speed would be on full display. It would also be the perfect field for starting quarterback Robert Haygood, who was from nearby East Point, Georgia, and looked to impress the hometown crowd.

A crowd of 43,424 was on hand to see if the Yellow Jackets could ruin Pitt's run to the top. They found early on that they could not. The victory by the Panthers was thorough and complete. Even punter Larry Swider had a big day, with punts of 60 and 77 yards in the contest. They started early with Dorsett, who had 113 yards on 27 carries, running in from 6 yards out to forge ahead, 7–0, and giving him the all-time school record for scoring. The Panthers then took advantage of a Wilamowski fumble recovery at the Georgia Tech 39, where Dorsett once again scored to push them ahead, 14–0. Tech cut the lead in half, then the Panthers lost Haygood for the season when he tore ligaments in his left knee. Luckily, they had Cavanaugh in reserve. He gave them the passing element that Majors was looking for.

After the teams traded touchdowns and with Pitt holding a 21–14 lead, Cavanaugh showed off his passing ability, hitting Jones down the middle for a 51-yard TD pass to restore their 2-touchdown lead. They made it 35–14 after a 26-yard pass to Jones was a prelude to a 10-yard Dorsett touchdown run. A Felder interception set up Cavanaugh's second touchdown pass of the evening to Jones, finishing off the home team in a 42–14 annihilation.

Despite the fact that the Panthers lost such a talented player in Haygood, Cavanaugh gave them an element that was missing in their veer offense. The Panthers were now a much more difficult team to beat.

GAME THREE

THE UNIVERSITY OF PITTSBURGH PANTHERS 21
THE TEMPLE UNIVERSITY OWLS 7
PITT STADIUM
SEPTEMBER 25, 1976
RECORD: 3-0-0

In the Johnny Majors era, Pitt had never started the season 3-0. In 1976, they would get the opportunity against their cross-state rivals, the Temple Owls. Coach Wayne Hardin, who had made some questionable comments in the past about the Panthers, took his Owls into this contest against the Panthers undefeated, with victories over Akron and Grambling State. While they weren't victories over elite programs, he hoped the experience would help make it a competitive contest.

The Panthers had vaulted from fourth to third in the United Press International poll to match their ranking in the AP, behind only Michigan and Ohio State, and Coach Majors was thrilled with the effort his team gave the first two games, especially from his seniors. "I haven't heard anyone on this team say they're satisfied yet. I believe this team has the ability to temper its confidence."[68] Despite the fact that starting quarterback Bobby Haygood was now lost for the season, Majors felt that his depth was better in 1976 and that the team's attitude would keep them winning.

One decision that Majors and his offensive coordinator, Joe Avezzano, had to make was who the backup quarterback would be. The choice involved Tom Yewcic, Wayne Adams, Woody Jackson, Dave Migliore and Randy Bentley. There seemed to be a significant dropoff between the starter and the five candidates for the backup role. If Cavanaugh was injured, it meant that some adjustments to the veer would likely need to be made.

The team they were facing, the Temple Owls, were on a seven-game winning streak stretching into 1975. Most of the victories came against inferior competition, and their last loss was the 55–6 debacle against Pitt, so few observers were giving them a chance against the Panthers. In fact, there was no line on the game in Las Vegas by famed prognosticator Jimmy "The Greek" Snyder. Hardin felt his team was still at least three years away from competing against the likes of Pitt and didn't appear confident himself. As it turned out, Hardin had his team ready for play and challenged the Panthers to an extent they hadn't been all season. Defensively, he decided not to be as aggressive as Notre Dame and Georgia Tech had been against the Pitt veer, playing almost a zone against it—playing "soft," as it was described in the *Pittsburgh Press*.

In the first quarter, after Pitt drove deep into Temple territory to begin the game, Carson Long missed a 30-yard field goal. Then disaster struck when Swider had a punt blocked and the Owls ran it in to go ahead, 7–0.

Dorsett was on the bench for part of the first half after suffering a bruised thigh, and the Panthers could muster only 2 Long field goals of 50 and 33 yards. Pitt went into the locker room behind for the first time all year, down 7–6.

Majors focused his team during halftime, and Dorsett's leg was feeling better after some ice treatment in the locker room. Walker and Dorsett (the latter ended up with 112 yards, his tenth consecutive 100-yard contest) ran for 60 of the 82 yards on a drive that ended with Walker scoring on a 1-yard run to put Pitt up, 12–7. Dorsett added 2 more points on the conversion, making it 14–7.

Bob Jury then picked off a fourth-quarter pass that was batted in the air by Cecil Johnson and Leroy Felder. Cavanaugh hit Jim Corbett for a 20-yard completion, and then Hutton ran for 11 more, setting up a 3-yard touchdown run by Dorsett to put the game away, 21–7.

Despite the unexpected closeness of the score, the Panther defense was dominant, holding the Temple offense to only 142 yards while forcing 3 turnovers.

There may not have been excitement at Pitt Stadium, but in Columbus, Ohio, Missouri shut out Ohio State in the second half while scoring twice to upset the second-ranked Buckeyes, 22–21, setting a path where Pitt would now become the second-ranked team in the country as they prepared to play at Duke the following week.

GAME FOUR

THE UNIVERSITY OF PITTSBURGH PANTHERS 44
THE DUKE UNIVERSITY BLUE DEVILS 31
WALLACE WADE STADIUM, DURHAM, NORTH CAROLINA
OCTOBER 2, 1976
RECORD: 4-0-0

Remarkably, the University of Pittsburgh now had the second-ranked team in the country in the Associated Press poll (third in the UPI behind Michigan and UCLA) following the combination of a victory over the Temple Owls and the shocking loss by Ohio State to the Missouri Tigers. They had their third road game of the season against the Duke Blue Devils, and on a fine evening in Durham, Matt Cavanaugh would show the college football nation that Pitt now had the potential for a devastating pass attack to go with the phenomenal assault on the ground as he displayed one of the great passing performances in Pitt history.

The Panther veer struggled somewhat against Temple, with the Owl defense playing almost a zone against it, waiting for the play to develop rather than the aggressive manner Notre Dame and Georgia Tech played against it. Majors claimed that he was afraid the Temple approach to the veer was a blueprint for how to defeat his team, as it turned out he made some adjustments that would confuse his opponents the rest of the campaign.

The team once again was relatively heathy, with Dorsett fully recovered from his bruised calf and Bob Jury playing despite a fractured bone in his hand. Carson Long had missed practice during the week to attend the funeral of his high school coach, Bob Oravetz, but would be ready to play on Saturday.

They were playing a Duke team that had an effective rushing attack, averaging 235 yards per game, led by quarterback Mike Dunn and running backs Art Gore and Tony Benjamin. They stood at 2-1 coming into this contest. Duke had defeated Tennessee in the opener, a win that had

Shown in a New England Patriot uniform, Matt Cavanaugh, who enjoyed a thirteen-year NFL career with the Patriots, 49ers, Eagles and Giants, won two Super Bowls in the process. At Pitt, he saw action in 1975 but became entrenched as a starter in the third game of the 1976 campaign after Robert Haygood's injury, giving Pitt an effective passing option out of the veer. He was at his best in bowl games, being named the MVP of both the Sugar and Gator Bowls his junior and senior seasons. Cavanaugh was named as a First Team All-American in 1977. *Courtesy of the University of Pittsburgh Athletics.*

Volunteer fans calling for head coach Bill Battle to be fired and replaced by Majors. The Blue Devils beat Virginia but lost to South Carolina, 24–6, between wins.

The situation at Tennessee was deteriorating after a 1-2 start following a 38–28 loss to Auburn. The heat on Battle was getting intense. When asked if the job at his alma mater was in his future, the Pitt coach muttered: "I will not discuss the situation period. I have my own program to be concerned about. I have enough to occupy myself physically and mentally because of the challenge we have in Pittsburgh."[69]

It was a rumor that would persist throughout the campaign, unfortunately becoming reality by season's end. Nonetheless, Majors became adept at focusing his team throughout the season. In this contest, he and Avezzano came up with a game plan that thoroughly confused the Duke defense. For the first time in the Johnny Majors era, the pass became prominent when needed, just like he wanted, and Matt Cavanaugh looked like he was becoming a star. Majors had his quarterback pass out of a play-action pass series that had incredible results on this day.

It wasn't that Pitt went away from the run; Dorsett broke the 100-yard plateau for the twelfth straight time, running for 129 yards. But the victory came firmly on the arm of Cavanaugh. After Duke went down the field 75 yards on its first drive to take a 7–0 lead, Willie Taylor caught a pass and took it for a 66-yard touchdown to tie the game.

J.C. Wilson then blocked a punt that went through the end zone to give the Panthers a 9–7 lead just before the Pitt quarterback continued his phenomenal quarter. First, he threw his second TD to Taylor from 10 yards out before finding a wide-open Jim Corbett from 27 yards out to make the score 23–7. Corbett caught 6 passes for 165 yards in the contest. Cavanaugh finished his phenomenal half by completing a 37-yard pass to Gordon Jones in the corner of the end zone after a Jury interception to send the Panthers into the locker room ahead, 30–7. It was Cavanaugh's fourth touchdown of the game, tying the mark set by John Hogan and Ivan Toncic.

The third quarter saw the quarterback break the Pitt record with his fifth scoring toss, this one once again to Jones, from 24 yards out. Dorsett finally scored one himself on a 4-yard run to put the visitors up, 44–15. Duke scored 2 touchdowns as the Panther defense appeared tired, but Pitt held on to win, 44–31, and improved their record to 4-0-0.

Cavanaugh's numbers were phenomenal. He only threw 17 times but completed 14 passes for 339 yards, 5 yards short of Bob Bestwick's record 345 against Michigan State in 1951. Cavanaugh broke the school record with 370 total yards. He also gave Majors what he felt the team needed to be great: a passing attack.

GAME FIVE

THE UNIVERSITY OF PITTSBURGH PANTHERS 27
THE UNIVERSITY OF LOUISVILLE CARDINALS 6
PITT STADIUM
OCTOBER 9, 1976
RECORD: 5-0-0

After Matt Cavanaugh's incredible performance against Duke, for which he was named AP Back of the Week, the Pitt Panther offense now looked unstoppable as they returned to Pitt Stadium to face the Louisville Cardinals. It would be Dorsett who had a chance to add to his impressive résumé, as he was only 47 yards short of Ed Marinaro (4,669) for the second-most career rushing yards in NCAA history. The Panthers were second in both polls after UCLA tied Ohio State, 10–10.

Pitt was taking on a Louisville team that was on a two-game winning streak, having defeated Drake and Wichita State after an opening-day loss to Mississippi State. Coach Vince Gibson's offense was led by 1,000-yard runner Calvin Prince and Nathan Poole. The offensive attack was thin beyond those two. The season totals for quarterbacks Stu Stram and Roy Steger had trouble matching Cavanaugh's single-game performance against Duke.

Coming back to Pitt in this contest was the Cardinals athletic director, Dave Hart, who was trying to toughen the Louisville calendar by scheduling Pitt and Alabama in 1976. It was the same Dave Hart who had had such a disastrous 3-27 tenure as the Panthers' head coach between 1966 and 1968. He recalled his Pitt days before the contest, taking full blame for the team's performance during those seasons. "I just didn't get the job done at Pitt. But when I look back at it, I believe nobody could have worked harder or given more than we did."[70] It was certainly a different Panther program now than the one he inherited ten years before.

Pitt took the field as a 30-point favorite against the Cardinals, looking to become 5-0 for the first time since Jock Sutherland patrolled the sidelines in 1938. Even with the impressive circumstances the program was experiencing, in 1976, Dorsett put things in perspective when asked how it felt to be so highly ranked. "It's nice but you'll notice nobody is jumping up and down. Now the shoe is on the other foot. A few years ago Pitt had no ranking and no respect. I remember how it was always easy to get fired up when we played teams like Notre Dame, Southern Cal and Oklahoma."[71]

Now it was Louisville trying to focus against the highest-ranked team the school had ever faced. As excited as they were for the opportunity, Pitt was the superior team and showed it from the outset. Cavanaugh scored from 17 yards out to complete an early 54-yard drive before Long made it 10–0 not long after Felder dove on a fumble at the Cardinal 18. In the second quarter, the Pitt quarterback scored his second TD from the 6-yard line. Then the defense got their chance to score. Parrish grabbed Stram and spun him around before Wilamowski knocked the ball out of his hand. Johnson dove on it in the end zone for the touchdown, making the score 24–0.

With the game just about out of hand, Dorsett ran for 18 of his 130 yards on the day to pass Marinaro for second on the all-time NCAA rushing list.

Long eventually kicked a 30-yard field goal to make it 27–0, but then disaster struck. Perhaps the one man whom the team could not afford to lose—and that included Tony Dorsett—was Matt Cavanaugh. On the next series, he suffered a hairline fracture at the top of his left ankle. Pitt ended the half with a 27–0 lead, but their quarterback was lost for this game and, presumably, a few more. His backup, Dave Migliore, came in and was ineffective, giving way to Tom Yewcic, who did no better.

A fourth-quarter blocked punt gave the Cardinals their only points of the contest in a 27–6 defeat. Pitt's national championship hopes were now in question, as they would move on without an experienced quarterback. It was at this time that Tony Dorsett took his game to another level and Yewcic became a cult hero who would surprisingly keep their historic season headed in the right direction.

Game Six

The University of Pittsburgh Panthers 36
The University of Miami Hurricanes 19
Pitt Stadium
October 16, 1976
Record: 6-0-0

In facing the University of Miami, the Panthers were dealing with their biggest challenge of the season. It wasn't necessarily the Hurricanes that were a concern, but the fact that both Matt Cavanaugh and Robert Haygood were injured and unavailable for this contest. The depth at quarterback was not impressive and included two seniors, Dave Migliore and Tom Yewcic, both who played in the Louisville game after Cavanugh's injury, and freshmen Woody Jackson and Randy Bentley. All but Migliore played in the team's recent junior-varsity victory against Potomac State, with Yewcic being the most successful, throwing for 145 yards on 4 completions that included 55- and 70-yard TD tosses to JoJo Heath.

While Dorsett was a far superior player than either Haygood or Cavanaugh, the running back position had depth, whereas the team was thin at quarterback. The loss of Haygood and Cavanaugh was perhaps the most disastrous thing that could happen to the Panthers. There was talk of Majors switching back to the I formation and letting the running backs be the focus to avoid having an inexperienced quarterback run the option in the veer. But the Pitt head coach felt he could do that through the veer. He did decide to use the I formation at times and continued to do so with more frequency the next couple of weeks to keep defenses from concentrating on the outside to stop Dorsett.

Luckily for Pitt, Miami wasn't the toughest opponent they would face. After crushing Bobby Bowden and his Florida State team, 47–0, they were decisively beaten by Colorado and Duke. Miami played well against fifth-ranked Nebraska in a 17–9 loss. Offensively, quarterbacks E.J. Baker, who had a sprained wrist and was questionable, and Frank Glover were effective, while the running game was headed by future New York Giant Ottis Anderson, who finished the season with 918 yards. Defensively, Majors felt Miami was the most mobile defense Pitt faced, led by All-American candidate Eddie Edwards.

As the week went on, Johnny decided that Yewcic would start the game. Yewcic was a walk-on from Johnstown who didn't even appear in the team's media guide before the season began and hadn't been assigned an official number. Ironically, he was given the unluckiest number of them all: 13. He stood only five feet, eleven inches tall and weighed 183 pounds and was only the ninth-string quarterback at the beginning of the year. Now the team's national championship chances fell on him. It would either be the beginning of a memorable story or the end of one. Johnny Majors also decided that freshman Woody Jackson would be Yewcic's backup, leaping ahead of Migliore.

A funny thing happened to Pitt's now questionable national championship run. The quarterback without a scholarship played beyond anyone's hopes, and Tony Dorsett showed why he was the Heisman favorite. Yewcic exclaimed, "Five minutes before the game when I was warming up coach Majors asked me if I was ready to go and I said I'm as ready as I'll ever be."[72]

It was the stellar Panther defense that got things started. After Miami had an incredible goal-line stand to stop Dorsett from the 1-yard line twice, Felder sacked third-string quarterback George Mason for a 2–0 lead. Weatherington then picked up a fumble that led to a 3-yard run by the Heisman Trophy candidate and a 9–0 Pitt advantage.

The defense came to the rescue again following a Walker fumble at the Pitt 14. Felder picked off a pass in the end zone, which led to a Panther drive that was highlighted by a 38-yard completion from Yewcic to Corbett. Long ended it with his first of 2 consecutive field goals that made the score 15–0. Dorsett was having a wonderful game, gaining 101 yards in the first half. But perhaps his most impressive play came on a 40-yard screen pass late in the second quarter that gave Pitt a 22–0 advantage as the half came to an end.

Miami cut the lead to 16 points early in the second half, but a reverse deep in Hurricane territory led to a Willie Taylor 7-yard run, making the score 29–6. Miami then scored on a 70-yard touchdown pass to cut Pitt's lead once again. But after Pitt returned the kickoff to the 47, Dorsett put the game away with a 53-yard scoring run on a pitchout. The Panthers were up once again, 36–12.

The Hurricanes scored late, but Pitt won the contest, 36–19. Yewcic completed only 2 passes for 78 yards, but he was the leader on the field the Panthers needed. Dorsett finished with 227 of the team's 341 yards rushing thanks to the incredible blocking of fullback Bobby Hutton, who knocked down ten Miami defenders. Dorsett was only 152 yards short of Archie Griffin's all-time NCAA career rushing mark. It was a magnificent performance by the team. Majors was ecstatic after the game. "Our staff did the best job of planning for one game of any staff I've ever had. I bow very lowly to them. Tony Dorsett is a Heisman Trophy winner if ever I saw one, and I've never been prouder of a football player than I am of Tom Yewcic."[73]

Pitt's national championship run was stronger than ever. They knew now that they could win, no matter what the situation.

Game Seven

The University of Pittsburgh Panthers 45
The Naval Academy Midshipmen 0
Navy–Marine Corps Memorial Stadium,
Annapolis, Maryland
October 23, 1976
Record: 7-0-0

As Pitt faced the Navy Midshipmen, revenge should have been the focus after Navy had soundly defeated the Panthers, 17–0, the year before. And while Pitt got redemption with the victory, the game was remembered for something else in the annals of Pitt football. It was the day Tony Dorsett met his date with history and became the greatest runner, at least statistically, that college football had ever seen.

Perhaps the most frustrating loss in the Johnny Majors regime at Pitt was the 17–0 upset defeat at the hands of Navy in 1975. Going for revenge at

Navy–Marine Corps Memorial Stadium with the second-ranked team in the nation would have been enough of a reason for the Panthers to win impressively, but after Dorsett ran for 227 yards against Miami, he now had a reasonable shot at breaking Griffin's record there.

When Dorsett came to Pitt as a smallish yet talented running back from nearby Hopewell High School, Majors was hoping he had a back who could help the program win. Instead, Dorsett was on course to become one of the greatest runners to play the game.

Before Dorsett, Pitt didn't have a particularly impressive list of running backs in its history, except for College Football Hall of Fame member Marshall Goldberg, who had the school record for career rushing (1,957 yards). As the only Panther back to rush for 1,000 yards in a season, which he would accomplish four times in his career, it took Dorsett only a little over a season to break Goldberg's record in 1974.

The team he would face had defeated only Connecticut on the season, coming into this contest at 1-4 and having lost their previous three games. Coach George Welsh seemed accepting of the fact that the Heisman Trophy favorite would break the record against his team. "If he gets the record against us its only because we happened to be there at the right time. Unless he gets hurt, there's no way he can't beak that record. He can get that on his own. They wouldn't even have to block for him."[74]

The game went as expected, a rout, with the incredible Pitt defense holding Navy's offense to a mere 106 yards of total offense. Yewcic continued his improbable story by completing 8 of 10 passes for 97 yards. But it was the Panther senior running back who stole the show. After a 69-yard run by Elliott Walker gave Pitt a 24–0 lead going into the final quarter, Dorsett scored on a run of 21 yards, which set up his moment in history.

Tony Dorsett was about to be a college football icon, and icons don't enter the history books on 1-yard runs. They do so with flair, and as Dorsett toppled Griffin, he had flair and then some. Needing only 4 more yards for the historic mark, Tony was in the game when by all rights he should have been sitting on the bench, enjoying the afternoon with his teammates. Yewcic pitched the ball, and Dorsett ripped around the left side of his line from the Navy 32. With the 4 yards behind him, he continued to dance through the Midshipmen defense, cutting into the open for a spectacular 32-yard touchdown run as his teammates rushed the field, prompting the referee to toss a penalty flag. But they didn't care. This was history, the all-time NCAA leading rusher finishing with 180 yards on the day and 5,206 for his career, 29 more than the Ohio State legend.

It may have begun as Pitt's attempt to gain revenge for the 1975 upset loss, but in the end, the game was all about a moment that will live well beyond the final score.

GAME EIGHT

THE UNIVERSITY OF PITTSBURGH PANTHERS 23
THE SYRACUSE UNIVERSITY ORANGEMEN 13
PITT STADIUM
OCTOBER 30, 1976
RECORD: 8-0-0

The second-ranked University of Pittsburgh football team had amassed a 7-0 mark while winning four games on the road. They would be in the city of Pittsburgh for their remaining four contests, beginning this afternoon with a game against Syracuse.

The story the week before was Tony Dorsett passing Archie Griffin on the NCAA career rushing list. He now had the goal of becoming the first back in the history of the collegiate version of the sport to pass the 6,000-yard plateau, which would be tough with only four games left. With the way he had been playing the last two weeks, it no longer was out of the question. He was now a national star. The Pro Football Hall of Fame wanted the jersey that he wore against Navy, although he had already given it to friend and former Panther basketball star Dr. Mickey Zernich, who was also an Aliquippa native. President Gerald Ford, a star at the University of Michigan, the team ahead of the Panthers in the polls, wanted to meet Dorsett and coach Majors on the campaign stop he was making before the Syracuse contest. They met the president at Pittsburgh International Airport. Majors presented Ford with an autographed Pitt jersey.

With all the excitement, people wondered why the Panthers weren't drawing more fans to Pitt Stadium. It's a subject that currently dominates social media sites, with many claiming that an on-campus stadium would make the difference. Pitt Stadium was an on-campus facility, and the Panthers were enjoying success at a level they hadn't since 1937. They had averaged a little under 40,000 fans per game to this point, and the debate on what it would take to draw like other successful schools was a topic in the papers. The school was aggressively trying to bring more people in by instituting one-dollar youth tickets, hoping to get 50,000 fans for the game.

Despite being a 28-point underdog, Syracuse had been playing better after losing its first three games of the season. The Orangemen had won three of their previous four, including a 24–16 victory over Temple the week before. Second-year quarterback Bill Hurley was their best player, leading the team in both passing and rushing yards. Hurley was at his best when he played the Panthers.

The administration succeeded in attracting more fans to the contest with its promotion; 50,399 were on hand to see a game that was much more difficult for the home team than anyone imagined it would be. After Long hit an early field goal, Hurley connected with Don Magee on an 80-yard touchdown pass, and Syracuse took a 7–3 lead as the first quarter was coming to an end.

Dorsett and his teammates would not be denied after starting the next drive at their own 5-yard line. He had runs of 33 and 15 yards and capped the long drive with a 1-yard run to give the Panthers a 10–7 advantage at the half. Two Dave Jacobs field goals for the Orange saw them take a 13–10 lead midway through the third quarter. Many in the stadium feared a devastating upset.

The Panthers' Heisman favorite, who finished with 241 yards for the game and passed Randolph-Macon's Howard Stevens for the all-time NCAA mark in any division with 5,447 yards in his career, then went 33 yards on a pitchout for a score that put the Panthers up, 17–13. Long converted from 47 yards to give Pitt a touchdown lead at 20–13, but Hurley, who rushed for 112 yards and passed for 203 more to set the Syracuse single-game total offense record, would keep the Orangemen's hopes alive. While they threatened, the Panther defense came up with many great plays to thwart scoring opportunities for Syracuse, especially late in the contest.

The Panthers had forced two fumbles already, and on a fourth-and-1 at the Pitt 11-yard line late in the game, Joe Stone, an offensive lineman who came in the game to help on defense, recognized the audible Hurley was calling. The defense stuffed the play as the Panthers took over on downs. The Orangemen again drove down the field and were in position to score, thanks to a face-mask penalty, but Bob Jury ended that drive with an interception at the 21.

Finally, Pitt put the game away with a Carson Long 29-yard 3-pointer to make the final score 23–13. It would be the closest Pitt came to defeat in this perfect season, but great teams find a way to win when they're not playing their best.

GAME NINE

THE UNIVERSITY OF PITTSBURGH PANTHERS 37
THE UNITED STATES MILITARY ACADEMY CADETS 7
PITT STADIUM
NOVEMBER 6, 1976
RECORD: 9-0-0

There wasn't much to remember on the field when Pitt met Army in 1976 other than Matt Cavanaugh returning from his ankle injury in the 37–7 victory. It's what happened almost 450 miles away in West Lafayette, Indiana, that took center stage. There, a 3-5 Purdue Boilermaker squad upset Michigan, the number-one team in the nation, 16–14, sending Pitt Stadium into hysterics. On that day, the Panthers finally ascended to the top spot in the polls.

Army was a better team than their Navy brethren. They came into the contest at 4-4 with a win over Stanford and a close loss to North Carolina, 34–32. But the Cadets had lost three of the previous four games, defeating only Air Force, 24–7. Led by quarterback Leamon Hall, Army had one of the better passing offenses in the nation. But defensively they were allowing 256 yards per game on the ground, which seemed perfect for Tony Dorsett and the Panther rushing attack, despite the fact that Dorsett injured his eye against Syracuse and had a bruised thigh and sore elbow, and Elliott Walker had been seen wearing a knee-high cast after spraining his ankle.

There were two main questions in the week before the game: Could Matt Cavanaugh come back this week from his ankle injury? And, which bowl would Pitt choose? With a win over Army almost a certainty, the three major bowls—the Orange, Sugar and Cotton—were lining up to recruit the Panthers. The Orange Bowl seemed the most aggressive, but all were in play if Pitt remained undefeated.

There were also rumors about teams wanting Johnny Majors as their coach. Atlanta Falcon owner Rankin Smith said in the press that he'd like to speak with the Pitt coach. And there were rumors about Majors returning to his alma mater, Tennessee, and that he had already agreed to become the Volunteers' coach at the end of the season.

A decent crowd of 45,573 showed up at Pitt Stadium to see Dorsett pull himself together despite the injuries and rush for 212 yards, keeping alive his quest to become the first NCAA back to reach 6,000 yards.

Yewcic's amazing performance as Pitt quarterback, one that earned him a scholarship, had come to an end after Cavanaugh returned following a Carson Long field goal in the first quarter to give Pitt a 3–0 lead. Majors said, "Tom Yewcic did a fine job for three weeks when we needed him, but Cavanaugh picked us up and loosened up Army, because they have to respect his arm. Matt is going to become one of the outstanding quarterbacks in the country."[75]

His entrance did loosen Army, as Long hit a 3-pointer from 39 yards before Dorsett scored 3 touchdowns and Cavanaugh tossed a 24-yard scoring strike to Willie Taylor. Long then knocked through his third field goal of the day in the 37–7 win. The field goal made Carson Long the NCAA's all-time career kick-scoring leader, with 244 points. But that feat was lost in the moment, as was the fact that Pitt dominated the contest. The Panthers outgained the Cadets, 519–225. In the forefront was what was going on in West Lafayette, Indiana.

In the Bo Schembechler era, which began in 1969, the only Big Ten team that Michigan lost to at that point was Ohio State. The Boilermaker running back Scott Dierking was having a career day, with 169 yards, and kicker Rick Supan had connected on a 23-yard field goal to put Purdue up, 16–14, with 4:20 left—certainly enough time for the Wolverines to respond. They drove to the Purdue 19 and lined up for a field goal with fourteen seconds left to win the game and most likely save their top ranking. Kicker Bob Wood's attempt was off target, and Purdue ran out the final nine seconds for the upset win. News of the final score was blared over the Pitt Stadium PA system, and the crowd and the players were ecstatic. Both started screaming, "We're number one! We're number one!"

Pitt now had a potential ninth national championship in their hands. If they won the final three games, it was theirs. Majors was also thrilled. "There's no doubt in my mind [that they were number one]. With this team, I'll take my chances with anybody. But it's nothing to sit on— we've still got to claw and scratch and block and tackle when we play West Virginia."[76]

With their two greatest rivals in front of them, this improbable four-year ride had reached a point that no one expected when Pitt hired Johnny Majors; they were now the best team in the country.

Game Ten

The University of Pittsburgh Panthers 24
The West Virginia University Mountaineers 16
Pitt Stadium
November 13, 1976
Record: 10-0-0

The Bobby Bowden era at West Virginia was now officially over. He had officially begun his historic tenure at Florida State. In his place was a man who would eventually make his mark on the game with an outstanding run at Indiana University of Pennsylvania, Frank Cignetti. After a 17–14 WVU upset in 1975, the Panthers were looking for revenge and to send Cignetti home a loser in his first Backyard Brawl.

Pitt had officially ascended to the number-one spot in the country after Michigan's upset loss to Purdue. And WVU was having a disappointing campaign, losing three of their previous four games to come into this contest at 4-5. But Majors knew that Pitt had to focus on the task at hand if they wanted to remain undefeated. "Michigan's loss shows that anybody can beat anybody on a given day."[77]

Offensively, Dan Kendra returned at quarterback and threw to an exceptional receiver in Steve Lewis. The trio at running back—Dwayne Woods, Walter Easley and Paul Lumley—was formidable but not spectacular. WVU's offense went on to be ranked 100 out of 137 schools by the year's end in points per game. It all had the look of another rout. Jimmy "The Greek" Snyder made the Panthers a 24-point favorite.

Pitt was fifth in the nation in scoring and eighth in total defense. Dorsett led the nation in yards per game and all-purpose yards and was second in scoring. Larry Swider was sixth in punting, and Bob Jury's 7 interceptions tied the school record and was third nationally at 0.8 interceptions per game.

As far as potential bowl games, the players had narrowed their choices to the Orange Bowl, which paid $1 million, and the Sugar, which would give the school $800,000 should they beat WVU. The *Pittsburgh Post-Gazette* was reporting that the players wanted the Orange Bowl by an almost three-to-one majority, but the decision was far from being made. Pitt had to defeat the Mountaineers if they hoped to make such a decision.

Statistically, it was every bit the rout Snyder expected, with Pitt outgaining WVU 399–169. But the Panthers also led significantly in a category they weren't interested in dominating: fumbles. The Panthers fumbled 8 times, losing 5; the Mountaineers conceded just 1 turnover, a Kendra interception. Luckily, the turnovers weren't the deciding factor; it only made the game more interesting.

The Panthers started the game with 3 passes before settling in on the ground. After being up only 7–3 in the first quarter on the heels of a 17-yard run by the Heisman Trophy favorite, Dorsett scored again in the second on a 3-yard scamper to make the Pitt lead 14–3 at the half. On the field at halftime, Dorsett received the ultimate honor, becoming the first player in school history to have his number retired. It was a fitting tribute for the school's greatest player to that time.

In the second half, Long increased the Pittsburgh lead to 17–3 with a 27-yard field goal before Kendra found Lewis from 14 yards out to cut the advantage to a touchdown. As the game was coming to an end, Dorsett appeared to be stopped on a pitchout, but he found a hole and sprinted 30 yards for a touchdown that put the game away, 24–10.

A lost fumble by Cavanaugh on the Pitt 34 helped make the game close, as WVU scored late to make it 24–16, but it was a case of too little, too late. The only excitement left was a questionable hit on Dorsett as time was running out, prompting the running back to throw punches and jam the ball into the helmet of WVU's Robert Meeley. Dorsett was ejected. Tony had 199 yards, bringing him 142 yards short of the 6,000 plateau. It was a goal that Joe Paterno and his Penn State Nittany Lions were planning on keeping him from in their next encounter. It would be the final step in Pitt's path to the national championship on New Year's Day.

AUTHOR'S NOTE: In 1976, the NCAA counted only regular-season statistics and not bowl stats in a player's official numbers. Currently, the NCAA counts bowls stats, which means that Dorsett would have actually eclipsed 6,000 yards against WVU midway in the contest when he crossed the 100-yard mark.

GAME ELEVEN

THE UNIVERSITY OF PITTSBURGH PANTHERS 24
THE PENN STATE UNIVERSITY NITTANY LIONS 7
THREE RIVERS STADIUM
NOVEMBER 26, 1976
RECORD: 11-0-0

The good news was that no matter how the battle between Pitt and Penn State turned out on the day after Thanksgiving at Three Rivers Stadium, the Panthers still had a spot in a major bowl, their first since the 1956 Sugar Bowl. The club had decided to accept a bid to play the University of Georgia on New Year's Day in the 1977 Sugar Bowl. Despite that, they still had one obstacle in front of them, their biggest albatross over the past decade: defeating a Joe Paterno–led Nittany Lion team.

In the previous couple of weeks, there were rumors that the Pitt players preferred to go to the Orange Bowl by a significant margin. But when Johnny Majors sat his leaders in a room and explained to them that playing the SEC champion University of Georgia gave them a much tougher opponent and an opportunity to capture the national championship than playing one of the five Big Eight opponents that were tied for the championship, the players decided unanimously that New Orleans is where they would be going and accepted the Sugar Bowl bid. It was important that Pitt take on the best opponent possible, as critics of their national championship hopes pointed to a schedule that might not have been as difficult as some of their competitors, especially as college football fans were looking forward to number two UCLA facing the third-ranked Trojans of USC. Southern Cal won that game and moved closer in the polls to the Panthers. If Pitt wasn't impressive against Penn State or took on an inferior foe in their bowl game, there was a chance that USC could jump over them, even if the Panthers went undefeated.

It was bad enough that Pitt was going up against the sixteenth-ranked team in the nation, but the Panthers were also having to face the thought that their coach might leave at the end of the season. It had been announced that the coach of Tennessee, Bill Battle, had resigned, and rumors that had circulated throughout the season were now becoming more intense. But it was tough, especially when Cas Myslinski admitted that he was contacted by Tennessee to speak with Majors and received his permission. Majors's main goal was to keep his team focused amid the reports. After all, Penn State was a team that Pitt hadn't beaten since 1965, before Joe Paterno got there. And until Pitt lost 7–6 the year before, the Panthers had never even come close.

Penn State came into this game a 1-touchdown underdog in an unusually tough season for Paterno, with his team only at 7-3. But they had played well, winning their previous six contests after a difficult 1-3 start. This made Panther fans nervous, especially after Nittany Lion quarterback Chuck Fusina found Bob Torrey on a 21-yard pass that Torrey ran in after catching it in the flat to give Penn State an early 7–0 advantage. Dorsett scored on a

To the left is Three Rivers Stadium in Pittsburgh. In 1976, after ten straight losses to Joe Paterno, the Panthers finally defeated Penn State, 24–7. Tony Dorsett ran for 224 yards that evening, becoming the first player to run for 6,000 yards in a collegiate career (in the days before the NCAA recognized bowl statistics as official stats). Bob Jury had 2 interceptions that evening, and Carson Long added a 47-yard field goal in the win that sent the Panthers to the Sugar Bowl and retaining their number-one ranking. *Courtesy of the University of Pittsburgh Athletics.*

6-yard run in the second quarter to tie the game. It looked like a long shot for Dorsett to break the 6,000-yard barrier after he was contained in the first half. (See the author's note at the end of the description of the WVU game.) Majors needed to make adjustments in the locker room, and he did just that.

Pitt went to an unbalanced line and then ran Dorsett as a fullback in the I formation, which surprised Penn State. As the third quarter was coming to an end and the Panthers had the ball at midfield, Dorsett slammed through the middle, powering through the Lions defense for 7 yards. On the next play, he took off on a 40-yard run that gave Pitt its first lead of the night.

The Heisman hopeful was having a tremendous second half, finishing the game with 224 yards, including an exciting 10-yard scamper as the third quarter came to an end to eclipse 6,000 yards for his career. Walker then ran in from 12 yards out for the score. Carson Long made amends for his difficult 1975 performance against Penn State with a 47-yard field goal that put the game out of reach, 24–7. With the defense playing tough, led by Jury's 2 interceptions, it was apparent that the Lions were done.

It was a great night that saw the Panthers break their long jinx against Penn State and convinced the voters in the polls that Pitt was the best team in the country. They would now go to the Sugar Bowl, where all they had to do was beat Georgia for this magical four-year ride to have its proper conclusion.

Chapter 9

1977 SUGAR BOWL

PITT IS IT

*I*t was both a joyful and an upsetting time as Pitt prepared for the 1977 Sugar Bowl. On the positive side, Tony Dorsett was about to become the first player in school history to capture the Heisman Trophy. On the other side, the rumors of head coach Johnny Majors leaving the Panthers to return to his alma mater in Tennessee appeared to be true.

The race for the Heisman, one that Dorsett finished fourth in the year before, ended up being a one-sided affair. The Aliquippa native secured 701 of the 863 first-place votes to win the award by 1,011 votes over his nearest rival, Ricky Bell of Sothern California. Michigan's Rob Lytle finished third. It was an honor not only to win the award but also to do so in such a significant manner.

Johnny Majors was in New York for a couple of reasons, not only to see his star back receive the Heisman but also to pick up the Lambert Trophy for Pitt. Reports said not only that he had accepted the job with the Volunteers, but also that there was a list of potential candidates to replace him at Pitt, including Frank Burns of Rutgers; George Welsh; and Jackie Sherrill, who had left before the season to be the head coach at Washington State. There was also a story that the school was trying to coerce the retired Ara Parseghian back into coaching, but the Hall of Fame coach quickly denied the rumors, saying he had no intention of returning to coaching.

Finally, on December 3, Majors pulled his players into the locker room to tell them that he was in fact leaving for Tennessee. It wasn't a financial decision; by all accounts Pitt was offering more money with the salary and his television show. For Majors, it was a chance to go home. "This may sound

Left: Pictured is the program for the 1976 battle between Penn State and Pitt at Three Rivers Stadium. It was the third of three consecutive games in the rivalry at Three Rivers. ABC-TV dictated that the game be moved there so that the network could utilize the facility's lights for an evening game. (Pitt Stadium and Beaver Stadium lacked lights.) Pitt won this contest, 24–7, to send the Panthers to the Sugar Bowl with a shot at the national championship. *Courtesy of David Finoli.*

Right: Pictured is the program for the 1977 Sugar Bowl between Pitt and Georgia. The Panthers dominated the fourth-ranked Bulldogs, pushing to a 21–0 halftime lead on the strength of touchdown runs by Matt Cavanaugh and Tony Dorsett and a 59-yard pass from Cavanaugh to Gordon Jones. Carson Long added 2 field goals in the second half as Pitt played their best game of the year in a 27–3 win to capture the school's ninth national championship. *Courtesy of David Finoli.*

corny or sentimental, but there are some roots that I have there. Finances were not involved, period. I think this was the year for me to decide to put some roots down somewhere. But when you're enjoying where you are.... Pittsburgh's a city I love and it's not easy to leave."[78]

The players seemed upset, but under Majors they had learned to become winners and took the news well. Many had hoped that Myslinski would choose Sherrill to come back to lead the program. But selecting a coach would be much easier this time around, with the program now considered one of the elite in the country.

As Cas was looking for a replacement, Majors had the opportunity to coach one more game for the university in an attempt to lead them to the national title. Myslinski made short work of his coaching search. He decided that the best man for the job was one who had left the year before: Jackie Sherrill. He lured the thirty-three-year-old coach back from Washington State, where the Cougars were 3-8 in his only season. The Pitt players were happy with his decision. Jackie decided that he wanted to keep any member of the staff who wanted to stay, but he also would bring in some very talented coaches: future Hall of Fame Coach Jimmy Johnson, who would be his assistant head coach; the man who replaced Sherrill in 1982, Foge Fazio, as defensive coordinator and linebackers coach; Dave Wannstedt, to be his strength and conditioning coach; and Joe Moore, who went on to become the preeminent offensive-line coach in the country.

With the coaching situation finalized, the team could focus on playing the Georgia Bulldogs in the Sugar Bowl. It was appropriate that Vince Dooley and the Bulldogs would be the opponent in this game. After all, it was in Athens, Georgia, in 1973 that the Majors era began with a surprising tie against the home team. The era would end against them on New Year's Day. "When I look back to our first game four years ago," Majors recalled, "I always feel something inside. Many people don't realize to this day what that Georgia game meant to us. The coaches and the players and all of us who started out at Pitt together. We were really in the dark, not knowing what type of team we had. Most of our players had been long-time losers and we weren't sure how our freshmen would pan out."[79]

Like Majors, Dooley had built Georgia into a powerhouse, capturing the Southeastern Conference with a 10-1 mark, losing only to Mississippi, 21–17, and securing a number-five ranking in the final regular-season Associated Press poll and finishing fourth in the UPI.

They were led by two quarterbacks, Matt Robinson, considered a better passer, and Ray Goff, who threw only 29 times but ran for 724 yards on the year. At running back, Kevin McLee broke the 1,000-yard barrier with 1,058, and Al Pollard chipped in 680.

The ways Dooley and Majors prepared their teams were vastly different. Dooley, who shaved his head bald before the game as a promise to his team, had a strict adherence to schedules and practices, with an 11:00 p.m. curfew, leaving the players little time for fun. Majors felt that his players deserved to enjoy the New Orleans nightlife, so he gave them a 2:00 a.m. curfew through the Wednesday before the contest before cutting it back each night leading up to the game. Dooley explained why he was stricter, saying simply that they were more conservative because Georgia was a southern school. Pitt came out loose, and the Bulldogs were a little tight as the game was about to begin.

After being named an Honorable Mention All-American in 1975 and a Second Team All-American a year later at guard, Tom Brzoza moved to center his senior season. He was spectacular at his new position in 1977 and garnered consensus First Team All-American honors that year. *Courtesy of the University of Pittsburgh Athletics.*

A Sugar Bowl record crowd of 76,117 showed up to the Superdome to see if the Panthers could handle their toughest opponent of the season. Champions are at their best when the game means the most, and Pitt was up to the challenge, playing their best game of the season. The team was completely focused after being abused in the hotel by the Georgia fans all week. "The fans were calling us dog food all week," Dorsett stated. "We just wanted to get out there and show them what was really dog food."[80]

Pitt's stars shined both offensively and defensively. Dorsett rambled for 202 yards; the game's MVP, Matt Cavanaugh, threw for 192 yards in a one-sided affair. Pitt outgained the Bulldogs, 480–181. By halftime, it was apparent who was going to win this contest. The onslaught started when Cavanaugh scored from 6 yards out, jumping in the end zone into the arms of his joyous teammates, setting up the famed *Sports Illustrated* cover shot. He then hit Jones on a 59-yard TD pass before Dorsett scored his touchdown, giving Pitt a 21–0 lead at the half.

In the second half, the defense continued to shine. After a Walker fumble deep in Pitt's own territory, Georgia could not move and scored their only points of the day on a field goal. Long would add two more field goals to his tremendous career. The Panthers proved to the college football world that they were number one in the 27–3 victory.

Left: Before becoming one of the greatest quarterbacks in NFL history with the Miami Dolphins, Dan Marino was leading the Pitt Panthers to national prominence. A hometown hero who grew up within walking distance of Pitt Stadium, Marino set the all-time single-season and career passing marks at the school while directing Pitt to two number-two rankings. *Courtesy of the University of Pittsburgh Athletics.*

Right: One of the byproducts of the successful program Majors created at Pitt was the opportunity to recruit better players. In 1977, Pitt had the opportunity to recruit Hugh Green. When discussing the greatest players in the program's history, the only two in the discussion are Green and Tony Dorsett. Green holds the all-time school sack mark with 49. He finished his career as a three-time consensus All-American, finishing second in the Heisman race in 1980. *Courtesy of the University of Pittsburgh Athletics.*

A few days later, they were officially named national champions to complete the four-year odyssey by Majors. Of course, he went on to Tennessee, and Sherrill kept the winning going with a 50-9-1 mark in his time at Pitt before tougher academic restrictions once again ended the program's championship era. While the program struggles today to approach the success it enjoyed back then, Panther fans can always take heart that there has never been such a magnificent turnaround as the one Majors produced between 1973 and 1976.

One of the great players in the era following Johnny Majors was linebacker Rickey Jackson. He was always overshadowed by Hugh Green while at Pitt but was selected as a Second Team All-American in 1980. In the NFL, Jackson had a much better career than Green, eventually being selected to the Pro Football Hall of Fame. *Courtesy of the University of Pittsburgh Athletics.*

NOTES

Chapter 1

1. John Antonik, "The Big Four," WVU 125, 2015, http://66.118.64.36/125/JA-61716.html#page-top.
2. Dick Fontana, "Pitt Hunting New Coach after Dave Hart Resigns," *Latrobe (PA) Bulletin*, November 26, 1968, 16.
3. Antonik, "Big Four."
4. Ibid.
5. *Pittsburgh (PA) Press*, "Carver Steps Down as Pitt AD," December 24, 1968, 14.
6. UPI, "Frank Kush Gets Challenge of Pitt's Coaching Position," *Latrobe Bulletin*, January 6, 1969, 12.
7. Pitt Football 1971 Media Guide, "Carl A. DePasqua," 13.
8. Bill Heufelder, "Kush Not Interested in Panther Job," *Pittsburgh Press*, November 28, 1972, 37.

Chapter 2

9. Marino Parascenzo, "DePasqua Fails Math in Pitt Shakeup," *Pittsburgh (PA) Post-Gazette*, November 28, 1972, 21.
10. Bill Heufelder, "Majors Coming to Pitt?," *Pittsburgh Press*, December 14, 1972, 72.

11. Marino Parascenzo, "Majors Shows Up at Pitt as Enthusiasm Crackles," *Pittsburgh Post-Gazette*, December 20, 1972, 22.

12. Ibid.

13. *Pitt Football 1973 Media Guide*, "A MAJOR Change to Pitt Football," 13.

14. Joe Starkey, "Class of '73 Keyed Pitt's Magical Season," Trib Live (Pittsburgh, PA), August 27, 2006, https://archive.triblive.com.

15. *Paths of Glory*.

16. Ibid.

CHAPTER 3

17. Ibid.

18. Marino Parascenzo, "Majors. Red-Letter Day," *Pittsburgh Post-Gazette*, April 6, 1973, 12.

19. Russ Franke, "Panthers Spirited in First Scrimmage of Spring," *Pittsburgh Press*, April 8, 1973, 70.

20. Marino Parascenzo, "Pitt Coach Has Words of Caution," *Pittsburgh Post-Gazette*, May 5, 1973, 7.

21. Starkey, "Class of '73 Keyed Pitt's Magical Season," Trib Live.

22. Ibid.

23. *Paths of Glory*.

24. Ibid.

25. Russ Franke, "New Look Pitt Ties Georgia 7–7," *Pittsburgh Press*, September 16, 1973, 69.

26. Russ Franke, "Pitt Shakes off Loss, Set for Northwestern," *Pittsburgh Press*, September 25, 1973, 27.

27. Russ Franke, "Coaching's a Dog's Life, Pitt's Majors Discovers," *Pittsburgh Press*, September 26, 1973, 68.

28. Pat Livingston, "Tony: Award Winner," *Pittsburgh Press*, 10/3/1973, 76.

29. Pat Livingston, "Pitt Can Play with Penn State—Navy's Welch," *Pittsburgh Press*, October 24, 1973, 76.

30. Bill Heufelder, "Kicking Worth Long Green," *Pittsburgh Press*, October 31, 1973, 44.

31. Marino Parascenzo, No Pitt Fatheads—Please," *Pittsburgh Post-Gazette*, November 1, 1973, 14.

CHAPTER 4

32. Pat Livingston, "Panthers Need 'Hot Sticks,'" *Pittsburgh Press*, December 13, 1973, 59.
33. Marino Parascenzo, "Not Going to Ole Miss, Majors Says," *Pittsburgh Post-Gazette*, December 18, 1973, 18.

CHAPTER 5

34. *Pittsburgh Post-Gazette*, "Pitt Signs Seven JC Recruits," March 15, 1974, 16.
35. *Pitt Football 1974 Media Guide*, "1974 Outlook," 14.
36. Russ Franke, "Long's Field Goal Saves Panthers," *Pittsburgh Press*, September 15, 1974, 67.
37. Russ Franke, "Pitt to Get Pepper Dose," *Pittsburgh Press*, September 17, 1974, 28.
38. Marino Parascenzo, "Did SC Soften Pitt for NC?," *Pittsburgh Post-Gazette*, October 7, 1973, 5.
39. Russ Franke, "Will Walker Join Dorsett?," *Pittsburgh Press*, October 9, 1974, 64.
40. Parascenzo, "Did SC Soften Pitt for NC?"
41. Joe Grata, "WWVU Coach Cites 'Cheap' TD," *Pittsburgh Press*, October 1974, 6.
42. Axelrod, Phil, "BC Gets Third Degree Burn from Pitt Speed," *Pittsburgh Post-Gazette*, October 21, 1974, 23.
43. Ibid.
44. Bill Christine, "Has Paterno Aroused Medwid?," *Pittsburgh Post-Gazette*, November 26, 1974, 16.
45. Ibid.

CHAPTER 6

46. *Pitt Football 1975 Media Guide*, "Look For Just About Anything," 8.
47. Phil Musick, "Homesick Elliott Walker Ponders Move to Miami," *Pittsburgh Post-Gazette*, February 23, 1975, 70.
48. Livingston, Pat, "A Major Economy Problem," *Pittsburgh Press*, August 5, 1975, 22.

49. Franke, Russ, "Pitt Needs Better Takeoff to Make Veer Fly—Majors," *Pittsburgh Press*, October 1, 1975, 57.

50. Phil Axelrod, "Majors Is Veer(y) Touchy About Veer," *Pittsburgh Post-Gazette*, October 2, 1975, 21.

51. Phil Axelrod, "Pitt's Defense Rests after Winning Case," *Pittsburgh Post-Gazette*, October 6, 1975, 17.

52. Ibid.

53. Russ Franke, "Pitt Defense Thinking Shutout Against Owls," *Pittsburgh Press*, October 7, 1975, 23.

54. Russ Franke, "Majors Won't Veer from Pitt Offense," Pittsburgh Press, October 8, 1975, 56.

55. Russ Franke, "Pitt Expected to Snap Army 'Bone,'" *Pittsburgh Press*, October 15, 1975, 67.

56. Phil Axelrod, "WV Dream Bursts," *Pittsburgh Post-Gazette*, October 13, 1975, 20.

57. Phil Axelrod, "Panthers Regroup after the Big Fall," *Pittsburgh Post-Gazette*, October 28, 1975, 11.

58. Ibid.

59. Pat Livingston, "Dorsett Isn't Paterno's Only Worry," *Pittsburgh Press*, November 19, 1975, 82.

60. Russ Franke, "Panthers, Long Fall Short, 7–6," *Pittsburgh Press*, November 23, 1975, 69.

Chapter 7

61. Pat Livingston, "Panthers Ahead of Schedule," *Pittsburgh Press*, December 21, 1975, 64.

62. Russ Franke, "Pitt Attack Runs on Solar Energy," *Pittsburgh Press*, December 27, 1975, 6.

Chapter 8

63. "Pittsburgh," *Street and Smith 1976 Football Annual*, 42.

64. Pat Livingston, "National Champs? Pitt? Who Knows?," *Pittsburgh Press*, March 9, 1976, 20.

65. Phil Axelrod, "Irish Bookends Hungry," *Pittsburgh Post-Gazette*, September 9, 1976, 14.

66. Phil Axelrod, "Irish Grass Green and High For Pitt," *Pittsburgh Post-Gazette*, September 1976, 6.

67. Phil Axelrod, "Can Dorsett Again Embarrass Devine," *Pittsburgh Post-Gazette*, September 6, 1976, 21.

68. Russ Franke, "Majors Finds Age Can Mean Beauty," *Pittsburgh Press*, September 21, 1976, 33.

69. Marino Parascenzo, "Tennessee Battle Cry," *Pittsburgh Post-Gazette*, October 1, 1976, 11.

70. Phil Axelrod, "Louisville's Program Looking Up," *Pittsburgh Post-Gazette*, October 8, 1976, 13.

71. Phil Axelrod, "No. 2 Pitt Tries Till It's Hertz," *Pittsburgh Post-Gazette*, October 9, 1976, 6.

72. Russ Franke, "Pitt Zips To 'Greatest' Win, 36–19," *Pittsburgh Press*, October 17, 1976, 67.

73. Ibid.

74. Phil Axelrod, "Navy Sends S.O.S," *Pittsburgh Post-Gazette*, October 23, 1976, 6.

75. Russ Franke, "Panthers Cry 'No. 1', Beat Army," *Pittsburgh Press*, November 7, 1976, 67.

76. Ibid.

77. Russ Franke, "Michigan Loss Not Major News For Pitt," *Pittsburgh Press*, November 8, 1976, 21.

CHAPTER 9

78. Phil Musick, "Majors Quitting Pitt to Coach Tennessee," *Pittsburgh Post-Gazette*, December 4, 1976, 1.

79. Russ Franke, "Georgia Peachier in Majors' Eyes," *Pittsburgh Press*, December 27, 1976, 24.

80. UPI, "Dogged Panthers Silence Georgians," *Pittsburgh Press*, January 2, 1977, 72.

BIBLIOGRAPHY

NEWSPAPERS

Latrobe (PA) Bulletin
Pittsburgh Post-Gazette
Pittsburgh Press
Tribune Review (Pittsburgh, PA)
Washington (PA) Observer

MAGAZINES

Game Plan Football Annual
The Sporting News
Sports Illustrated
Street and Smith Football Annual

VIDEO

Paths of Glory: 100 Years of Pitt Football. Ross Sports Productions. WQED
   Multimedia. Pittsburgh, Pennsylvania, 2005.

BIBLIOGRAPHY

MEDIA GUIDES

Pitt Football Media Guide. University of Pittsburgh Athletics Media Relations Office, 1969–77.

WEBSITES

ACC.org
ESPN.Com
PittsburghPanthers.com
Triblive.com
WVU125.com

BOOKS

Finoli, David. *Pittsburgh's Greatest Athletes*. Charleston, SC: The History Press, 2019.

———. *Pittsburgh's Greatest Teams*. Charleston, SC: The History Press, 2017.

———. *When Pitt Ruled the Gridiron*. Jefferson, NC: McFarland & Company, 2014.

Finoli, David, and Chris Fletcher. *Steel City Gridirons*. Pittsburgh, PA: Towers Maguire Publishing, 2006.

Pittsburgh Post-Gazette. *The Year the Panthers Roared*. Louisville, KY: Ad Craft, 1996.

The Sporting News. *College Football's Twenty-Five Greatest Teams*. St. Louis, MO: Sporting News Publishers, 1988.

ABOUT THE AUTHOR

*D*avid Finoli is an author and sports historian who has written numerous titles on the history of sports in western Pennsylvania. He has written books for Arcadia Publishing and The History Press, including *Pittsburgh's Greatest Teams* and *Unlucky 21: The Saddest Stories and Games in Pittsburgh Sports History*. He also is a contributor to various books, magazines and sports websites. He lives in Monroeville with his family.

Visit us at
www.historypress.com